THE
INVISIBLE
DISEASE

Contents

poisoned by epoxy, and those of thousands of office employees around the world suffering from different illnesses, variously called electro-hypersensitivity, multiple chemical sensitivity, chronic fatigue, sick building syndrome, etc.

Introduction

The truth has been lying on the table for at least 20 years, in reality more. They who understood didn't say a word. Meanwhile thousands of people have been ridiculed and silenced. They will suffer also in the future because the truth will be denied for many years to come.

That's the story I tell in this book. The story of people who became sick in front of their computer screens at the beginning of worldwide computerisation. When they claimed that symptoms such as a burning sensation in the skin, lightsensitivity, numbness, dizziness, exhaustion, skin rashes and loss of memory had something to do with the new devices they were working with, doctors and authorities laughed at them and explained away everything using psychology.

In 1986, a man called Joseph LaDou visited Sweden. He was acting chief for the Division of Occupational and Environmental Medicine at the University of California School of Medicine in San Fransisco, California. Over many years he had raised the alarm about the major health problems in the microelectronic industry in Silicon Valley, health problems related especially to the semiconductor fabrication. Occupational exposure to chemicals, gases and other toxic materials had already resulted in a high occurance of occupational illnesses.

In Sweden a debate had been going on for some years about clusters of miscarriages and, from 1985, about a whole range of symptoms among computer users. But when Joseph LaDou met representatives from work safety authorities in Stockholm and also the Swedish Minister of Labor, Anna-Greta Leijon, and told them about the situation in Silicon Valley, no one seemed to have drawn any parallells to the problems in Sweden. Instead there has been a twenty-year discussion about the electromagnetic fields from computers and other electronic devices. Millions of Swedish crowns have been spent on radiation research, not many crowns on chemicals used in the devices, and not a single crown on possible synergistic effects of chemicals and radiation.

The chemical industry could lean back, satisfied by the direction of the debate. No one asked for information about which chemicals were being used in their products.

In front of me I have number 1, January-March 1986, of *Occupational Medicine*, edited by Joseph LaDou. The title is "The microelectronic Industry". Here you can read almost everything worth knowing in order to understand why people have become sick in a worldwide Silicon Valley syndrome.

Was this discussion misleading with regard to radiation? No, I don't think so. Already in Silicon Valley there were problems with radiation of different kinds such as uv and microwaves in combination with the chemicals. But there are many excellent books about electromagnetic radiation and more will come. I have not even tried to give any survey of the research in this area. Other, more talented, people will write about that. My book deals with people suffering from chronic symptoms that have been given different names in different countries. As a journalist I have tried to gather some pieces of this enormous puzzle.

The problem was that no one took notice of the chemicals in computer equipments, although in 1990 IBM was forced to admit that there were chemicals emitted from their devices in office use. Today, in Autumn 2003 when I'm writing this, there are lawsuits going on in USA against IBM. The plaintiffs are hundreds of IBM-employees who have been exposed to the chemicals used in the fabrication of chips, disks and other components and now are suffering from very serious illnesses. The next step is to address the continuing low-dose exposure from our computers and other electronics.

1

The evidence in front
of our eyes

When I began to take an interest in this issue, which has become increasingly complex, I was employed as a labor-market reporter at a union journal, TCO-*tidningen*, owned by the Swedish Confederation of Professional Employees, TCO.

Chance often plays a decisive role in our fate. One day, in October 1985, a lawyer from the occupational injuries department at TCO came into my room and told me that he had helped a 48-year-old female bank clerk to get her skin complaints acknowledged as an occupational injury, resulting from her using computer screens. Her doctor had written a certificate, stating that the changes in her skin were of the kind found following exposure to radiation, especially UV- and X-rays. According to him there was a clear connection with her work, but he was unable to state which item in the screen could be the cause of her skin complaint. The regional social insurance office in Stockholm had approved the occupational injuries claim.

Radiation injuries caused by computer screens! This was, of course, a sensation and the article I wrote attracted a lot of attention. The Swedish debate on health risks associated with working in front of computer screens had, up to that time, been about miscarriages and perhaps even cancer. Now it became apparent that for a number of years, several doctors across the whole country

1

had treated patients with different skin and eye complaints that they claimed were related to their working in front of computer screens. But the doctors had most often dismissed them, in many cases sending them to psychiatrists. The media had not taken notice of this. The situation changed as soon as the bank employee's injuries were classified as work-related. The first article I wrote about her started a deluge of phone calls and letters to the journal from all over Sweden. People who had no contact with one another told the same story: they felt as if they had been lying in the sun for too long, their skin felt burned and stretched, they could no longer face using their VDUs and some of them were forced to keep in the shade as they couldn't stand sunlight. They couldn't stand fluorescent lighting either. The latter was something they all talked about. What was this all about? My schooldays studies of physics and chemistry were only basic. I'd taken liberal arts and hadn't even dreamed of landing in this kind of situation.

It was difficult to ignore similar stories coming from so many people, even though the doctors and technicians that I interviewed one after the other told me that this was impossible. Computer display screens do not cause radiation injuries. Who then, had said that the bank employee had radiation injuries? Björn Lagerholm, a histopathologist, a senior physician at Karolinska Hospital's skin clinic in Stockholm, had written the doctor's certificate. Under a microscope he had studied skin biopsies from the woman and maintained that the changes he saw looked just like the ones he was familiar with from UV- and x-ray radiation.

A histopathologist is an expert on pathologic changes of the skin. Björn Lagerholm was one of the best in the field in the Nordic countries; an associate professor, popular with students, respected by colleagues and frequently entrusted with analytical commissions both in Sweden and abroad. As he also ran a private clinic he had studied more biopsies under a microscope than anyone else in the country. He was not happy with interviews and publicity but he did consent to my interviewing him – several interviews were to follow – as he knew that the journal I worked for represented the majority of white-collar workers who were increasingly working in front of computer screens. And he had, as he saw it, a duty to talk about what he had seen.

It soon became apparent that the bank clerk wasn't the only case. During the years prior to this case, Lagerholm had treated quite a number of patients, people of different ages – including some young men in their twenties. This had come as a surprise to Björn Lagerholm. They came to him with expanded facial blood vessels, sometimes swellings and blisters, and they complained about itchiness and a burning sensation, as if they'd been lying in the sun for too long. Many of them had skin changes of a kind usually called elastosis solaris, which occurs among seamen and farmers, after living most of their lives outdoors. All of these patients had a common background – they sat in front of VDUs in offices.

As a histopathologist, Björn Lagerholm took biopsies – skin samples – from his patients. During examination, patient-by-patient, he saw changes that are usually related to radiation. In 1986 he wrote an article about his observations in *Läkartidningen*, a Swedish medical journal.

A wave of fright spread throughout Sweden as early as October 1985. Authorities and technical experts hurried to explain that there wasn't any dangerous radiation emitted from computer screens. Björn Lagerholm commented that he wasn't a technician and couldn't say anything about VDUs, but as a doctor he didn't like it when technicians made cocksure statements about medical matters.

The Swedish Institute for Radiation Protection came to a quick decision to run tests using a life-size doll in front of a computer screen, to find out if the fields around screens could possibly carry what are called radon daughters, radioactive decomposition products from radon, to screen users. Perhaps Lagerholm's patients had happened to be sitting in buildings affected by radon radiation.

It was found that there were increased deposits of radon daughters on the doll and above all on the screen, which thereby gave off certain amounts of alpha radiation. But, in their report, the researchers at the Institute explained that no further investigation was required; the radiation wouldn't penetrate deeper than 0.08 millimeters into human skin. A few years later it was shown that this conclusion was somewhat hasty when a neurobiologist, Olle Johansson at the Karolinska Institute, found that there are nerve fibers only 0.01 to 0.04 mm below the surface of the horny layer of the epidermis in areas of thin skin such as that in the face.

Very soon after Björn Lagerholm's disclosures an effective cover-up of the entire issue of health risks related to using VDUs commenced. Remarkably enough, one of his colleagues, the late Professor Sture Lidén, was one of the contributors to this cover-up. To begin with Sture Lidén showed interest in getting the problem surveyed, initiating an extensive examination of the skin of almost 4000 randomly selected white-collar workers, members of TCO. They were given a questionnaire to answer – this was the world's first skin investigation to be carried out by questionnaire. At the same time, Professor Lidén became supervisor for assistant physician Mats Berg at Karolinska Hospital's skin clinic, who carried out this investigation and was later to use it as his doctoral dissertation. A lame protest was raised by TCO's lawyer specializing in occupational injuries: wouldn't it have been more justified to quickly carry out an investigation of the increasing number of cases in which serious symptoms had arisen rather than a group of randomly selected people? Perhaps it wasn't only the employees who should have been examined, but also the VDUs they had used. It was clear that those most seriously afflicted wouldn't be found by conducting an extensive epidemiological survey. In addition, time was being lost, time that should have been spent on more concrete measures.

When the TCO survey had been completed, it was found that twice as many VDU users had experienced mild sensory phenomena such as burning sensations, itching, and irritation as those in a control group. They had, however, been able to continue working. Sture Lidén didn't think this was a cause for concern: "Can't we all sense itching here and there if we think about it? If you read in the paper that you can get radiation injuries from using VDUs, naturally you get scared and feel you have symptoms." Together, Lidén and Berg told the media that everyone could stop worrying: Nothing indicated that there was anything dangerous about VDUs. They made a lot of noise about not finding any increase in the frequency of skin diseases. But was it known skin diseases that should have been looked for? These would have been found by an experienced dermatologist like Björn Lagerholm.

In Mats Berg's thesis for his doctorate, presented a few months later, a minor histopathological study of people who had problems in connection with VDUs, and a control group, was also included. No evidence was found that any skin changes could arise as a result of using VDUs. But the lead up to this study was somewhat unusual. As Mats Berg wasn't a histopathologist himself, he had given a number of skin biopsies to Björn Lagerholm and two other histopathologists at Karolinska Hospital for analysis under a microscope. Breaking the code, he told Björn Lagerholm that the biopsies that had changes happened to come from patients who had reported problems arising in connection with using VDUs. There were about fifty such cases. Shortly afterwards he explained to Lagerholm that he couldn't report these findings. This being so, Björn Lagerholm refused to sign Mats Berg's study from which his own findings had been omitted. For some reason, the skin samples disappeared.

A few years later, the question of the disappearance of these skin samples from Karolinska Hospital were raised in debate articles published in some major Swedish daily papers and in a TV program. On TV, Sture Lidén explained that it was a question of "uncontrolled studies that have been impossible to verify". Björn Lagerholm maintained that he had found specific changes "but, if they had been included in the survey, the results would, of course, have been different, it would have been necessary to review the entire investigation, causing a scandal. That's why they don't want to hear any more about it." No authority stepped in to clarify exactly what had happened at Karolinska Hospital. After a while everything was forgotten. Professor Sture Lidén went round the departments of occupational medicine in Sweden during the 1980s, trying to reach consensus on how to treat people who had medical problems connected to using VDUs. They should be told that research hadn't revealed any hazards and no one needed to worry. At most, people might get some acne rosacea, a reddening of the skin.

Acne rosacea was the diagnosis that doctors hurriedly came to from then on, sometimes without even seeing the patient. But Björn Lagerholm just scoffed: they didn't know what they were talking about, there are several different forms of acne rosacea, diagnosis wasn't all that simple. From what he had seen under his microscope, there was only some similarity between the skin changes in "VDU patients" and those who were suffering from acne rosacea, he declared when I interviewed him.

Swedish researchers became divided into two camps at an early stage, those who thought it was a question of real physical causes of the symptoms VDU users reported and those who thought it was a mental phenomenon. In the 1990s, Thomas Brante, Assistant Professor of Sociology at the University of Lund, described the scientific controversy in question. He saw the skin doctor Sture Lidén as the foremost proponent for the second school of thought, "he refines the psychiatric model".

Sture Lidén linked electro-hypersensitivity with multiple chemical sensitivity, which is especially widespread in the USA. He explained that both syndromes depend on conditioning. Under certain circumstances a person could feel reddening and warmth in his/her face, due to stress, and become increasingly aware of this, believing it to be something dangerous. In the end the autonomic nervous system started a reaction every time the person found him/herself in a similar situation.

Björn Lagerholm retired in 1993. In the same year the Swedish Medical Association held a discussion evening on VDUs and health, inviting Björn Lagerholm to give an account of his findings. But he didn't do so. He had retired from public life, which he had never enjoyed. It certainly isn't too wild a guess that he was also hurt by the fact that his competence had weighed so lightly in this matter. He didn't bother any more. He had reported what he had seen. There had been a conspiracy of silence. Now others had to take over. But he couldn't refrain from sending a note to the Medical Association. A short list of the "clear and distinctive" changes that he had observed in the skin of VDU patients – "own patients, about fifteen, and two to four hundred micro morphological analyses," i.e. analyses of the tiny structures and formations in skin.

The following is a little intricate, but I think it is worth the trouble to try to penetrate Björn Lagerholm's writings as they contradict the contention of other experts that there are no objective findings whatsoever resulting from the examination of skin from VDU patients. He wrote that he had found "clinical/ macro morphological changes" i.e. major changes, often to the whole of one side of the faces, necks and chest areas, shoulders, and upper arms of his patients. The changes had been similar in all areas, even micro morphologically, i.e. even in the tiny structures in the skin that he could see using a microscope.

In the epidermis, the top layer of skin, he had seen intracellular edemas (pockets of fluid) in the "stratum basale = altération cavitaire Leloir", i.e. in the bottom layer of the outer skin. He wrote that damage to the lysosomatic membranes (cell pockets that contain enzymes) give rise to this kind of edema. "UV or other short-wave radiation is a known cause," he adds. In corium papilla (small projections of tissue at the base of hairs) in the dermis, the deep inner layer of skin, as well as in the "stratum papillare" he had found that the threadlike components referred to as "squelettes élastiques Darier" were fewer than normal or completely missing. "According to Darier, the known cause is UV or other short-wave

radiation," he wrote. Neither of these two changes is usual in relation to acne rosacea, he explained. Moreover, he had found an
increased number of vessels, extended vessels and, above all, an
increased number of mast cells, which normally occur in connection with allergies and various types of inflammation. And
he pointed out that, here as well, there is a known cause of such
changes, namely UV and other short-wave radiation. He also indicated that this type of radiation sets free histamine from the
mast cells, a substance that can give rise to the type of symptoms
described by those who had used computer screens. They also
occur in bronchial spasms.

Much later, some researchers reported that microwaves of the
kind emitted by mobile phones double the production of histamine and that this type of electromagnetic radiation also lowers
the effects of medicines used against asthma. In other words, Björn
Lagerholm was first to talk about mast cells in a concrete context,
concerning patients who had been exposed to electromagnetic
fields in varying forms. I have never heard anyone criticize his
findings and diagnoses in public. But his daring to mention that
VDUs could potentially be hazardous for human skin was more
than our hi-tech society and some of his colleagues were prepared
to swallow. If it wasn't possible to question his competence they
could at least keep his findings quiet. Colleagues like Sture Lidén
avoided discussing the issue with him. But, in 1993, the Swedish
Medical Association wanted him to tell of his observations. Even
though he didn't care to put in an appearance, at least he took
the effort to write the summary of his observations. It was rather
typical of Björn Lagerholm that he couldn't refrain from ending
the summary with a quotation from Goethe: "Was ist das schw-
erste von allem ist zu sehen was for den Augen liegt." "The most
difficult thing of all is to see what is right in front of your eyes."

I wish that I'd been competent enough to evaluate everything that
was right in front of my eyes over all these years, not just Lager-

holm's comments but also those of many of the people who have been afflicted, research reports, notes I have made during interviews with experts, newspaper articles from around the world... I have a feeling that all the pieces of the puzzle are known. But, like Lagerholm's observations, they have been ignored or regarded as being most inconvenient.

Several years after Björn Lagerholm's first alarming finds of skin changes, the next piece of this puzzle was put on the table by Per Hedemalm, MSc (Engineering): it could be a question of interaction between light and chemicals.

If it is a question of combined effects of uv, ultraviolet light, and chemicals it means that Björn Lagerholm's observations may be explained by previously known mechanisms concerning sensitivity to light. He had noted that the skin changes were not found under the nose or chin, where light doesn't usually fall and that the skin changes often occurred only on one side of the face.

In autumn 2001 I phoned Björn Lagerholm to ask him what he thought about Per Hedemalm's hypothesis. "It's a very interesting suggestion, but unfortunately I don't know anything about chemicals," he answered.

Björn Lagerholm isn't the only dermatologist in the world to raise the alarm about the possible hazards of using vdus. In a dermatological journal Professor Alexander Fischer, a well-known New York skin specialist, in 1988 reported a case of a woman who had what he called "vdu dermatitis". Like Björn Lagerholm he did not hesitate to point to the use of vdus as a probable cause. He also referred to two other American doctors, Lawrence R. Feldman and William H. Eaglstein at the Department of Dermatology, University of Pittsburgh, who had raised the alarm as early as February 1985 in a letter to the *Annals of the American Academy of Dermatology*, referring to a new phenomenon, which they called "terminal illness." They had treated a 33-year-old male patient who had suffered from redness, burning, and itching on the upper sides of both hands and lower arms, mainly on the right side, for 15 months. He had noted this eruption two weeks after starting a new job, working at a computer terminal. The symptoms improved considerably over weekends when he was away from work.

When the doctors covered one of the patient's hands with a plaster called "Duoderm" while at work the area covered remained clear. This plaster is impenetrable; it is used in connection with serious burns. The two doctors did consider the possibility that some form of chemical emission was occurring from the screen or the surroundings, but despite extensive testing, they couldn't identify any cause. When they tested the patient using ultraviolet light B (UV-B), he developed a linear red streak over the right scapular area along a line where the drape covering the test area had slipped off. The doctors thought this was a phototoxic reaction (poisonous effect of light) but were unable to ascertain any general sensitivity to UV-B or UV-A, summarizing matters as follows: "We feel that another form of electromagnetic radiation emitted from the video display units is the most likely etiologic factor in this man's condition. We do not know the spectrum of radiation emitted from the VDU at his office."

Neither of these two doctors nor Alexander Fischer referred to any skin biopsies. They had obviously never taken any. The matching part of the "terminal illness" puzzle had been found in Sweden but was not published in any other way than in Björn Lagerholm's own debate article from 1986 in *Läkartidningen*, a Swedish medical journal. It is usually referred to in footnotes in summaries of Swedish research, if it is mentioned at all.

The first reports of skin complaints whilst working with VDUs had come from the UK as early as the beginning of the 1980s. In 1982, Arvid Nilsen, a dermatologist in Norway, had reported that some thirty women, working for a Norwegian telephone operator, had itching, burning rashes that disappeared over weekends when they were not at their workplace. He didn't recognize the symptoms as any skin complaint he had seen earlier. He eliminated acne rosacea, the diagnosis that later was to become so common in Sweden with respect to VDU-related skin complaints. But he, too, took no biopsies.

At the first international VDU Conference, held in Stockholm in 1986, I met Bob DeMatteo, a Canadian employed by the Ontario Public Service Employees Union. He told me that skin rashes were a common complaint among employees working in front of VDUs in Canada and the USA, not only among persons with fair skins but also those with dark or even black skin.

DeMatteo had brought a few copies of his book *Terminal Shock* with him. The second edition had just been published. In it he tells of other health problems related to working with VDUs: strange clusters of miscarriages among women from different workplaces, premature births and children born with deformities, cases of cataracts in the back part of the lens capsule in the eye, headaches, tiredness, sleeping problems... Cataracts, in particular, caught my attention. In his book, Bob DeMatteo wrote that many radiation-induced cataracts had been reported among VDU operators in North America, the first cases as early as 1977. Two *New York Times* copy editors, aged 29 and 35, had been diagnosed as having developed cataracts on the back surface of the lens capsule, a location that, according to DeMatteo, is an objective sign of radiation-induced injury. He mentioned that this particular kind of cataract is prevalent among people exposed to radio frequencies and microwaves. He also wrote that it had been known for many decades that electromagnetic radiation could produce cataracts. Medical data collected over the years indicate that radiation from certain areas of the electromagnetic spectrum, including x-ray, ultraviolet, infrared, microwave, and radio frequencies can initiate the formation of cataracts.

"Although many statements have been made denying that cataracts could have been caused by radiant energy from VDUs, they have not been based on any credible study whatsoever," Bob DeMatteo wrote.

In the book *Fältslaget*, published in Sweden in 1989, my colleague Carl von Schéele and I wrote about VDU operators in Sweden who had surprisingly been afflicted with cataracts of the very same kind, on the back surface in the lens capsule. We also wrote about cases of detachment of the retina, which had occurred in a remarkable manner.

> Shaul Buchnick, a 39-year-old computer programmer in Stockholm, was one of these cases. After working in front of VDUs for three years – as a consultant he had worked with screens made by various manufacturers – he began to have headaches and felt pressure in his left eye. He usually worked with two screens on his left. The trouble continued to get worse, culminating just before Christmas 1982. He was taken to hospital as an acute case of retina detachment was operated on four times but his sight couldn't be restored. At that time changes were also noticed in his right eye.
>
> When, later, he filed an occupational injuries claim his doctor wrote "the patient's condition has no connection to his using VDUs for many years." An eye specialist recommended that he could return to full-time work in front of screens.
>
> Then, in 1988, Shaul Buchnik began to have skin problems on the left side of his body when he started working with a new VDU. Pressure returned to his left eye. When he went home after having used the new screen for three hours he felt as if he had been sunburned on the left side of his upper body. He could hardly sleep. Itching persisted for two months. He could no longer stand fluorescent lighting and tried to avoid having any lamps switched on at home. A skin specialist diagnosed inflammation on the left side of his face. Another specialist, at the Hadassa Hospital in Jerusalem, talked about inflammation of nerves on the left side of Buchnik's face.

In his book, Bob DeMatteo tackles almost all of the issues that have slowly come to be of concern in Sweden over the years. For example, he discusses the interspersion of high-frequency radiation in emissions from VDUs and mentions that the chemicals used in devices may also be harmful.

Returning to the pilot case – the bank clerk – her case went very badly. The supervisory authority for the regional social insurance offices were quick to appeal when they found out that her occupational injury had been approved. Ten years of legal proceedings followed. In October 1994 the claim was rejected at the highest level.

When asked recently, Christina Eliasch, senior physician at the Stockholm Regional Social Insurance Office, said that the ruling was a miscarriage of justice. The case of the bank clerk should have been assessed in accordance with the earlier Swedish Occupational Injuries Law, which was valid up to 1993. After this time the requirements for proof became more stringent, she says. Instead, in practice, consideration was given in accordance with the new law. This ruling created a precedent that came to be of major importance for the thousands of employees in Sweden who now got the message: there is no point in filing an occupational injuries claim no matter what symptoms arise in connection with working with VDUs. We can simply note that they have been sacrificed on the altar of technology and that the praiseworthy safety net of Swedish social security has major flaws when it comes to new illnesses that have not been previously diagnosed.

Those afflicted started an association in 1987. They called themselves electro-hypersensitive to indicate that it wasn't only VDUs that they reacted against, even though 90 per cent of the members had fallen ill whilst using screens. Electro-hypersensitivity became the term that was most commonly used, embracing a number of neurological symptoms.

With the use of mobile phones, these symptoms have once

again become current. Now, new groups are affected. Those already afflicted following problems arising in connection with VDUs find it increasingly problematical to live in modern society. What is common to both VDUs and mobile phones? The most obvious answer is electromagnetic radiation and chemical emissions.

"We have hardly ever discussed high frequencies emitted from VDUs," writes Jan Kullberg, MSc (Engineering), who has been active in the Swedish Association for Electro-hypersensitive Persons:

> A computer and VDU emit a medley of frequencies from 50 hertz to one or more than one gigahertz (a thousand million hertz). The low frequency band, 0–400 kHz, forms a very small part of the whole spectrum of frequencies, less than one half per thousand. At present, conclusions about electro-hypersensitivity are largely drawn from observations concerned with this small fraction of the total picture. This seems to me to be completely meaningless.

Jan Kullberg's view is that, by focusing on low frequency fields when seeking explanations for VDU-related illnesses and electro-hypersensitivity, researchers "have looked for something under street lights because there is more light there".

Mobile phones have altered things. Researchers are currently concentrating interest on microwaves from cellular phones. But VDUs and their victims have been placed on hold, not to say completely forgotten. In England, records of the symptoms reported in connection with mobile phones have been collected. These include headaches, dizziness, ear pains, tinnitus, blurred vision, bloodshot eyes, and, sometimes, loss of vision, a burning sensation similar to sunburn on the face, neck, and eyes, as well as numbness. Many, even young people, complain of loss of short-term memory and a feeling of exhaustion is common. All this could as well have been described by VDU-users. People who have carried mobile phones next to their bodies have noticed traces of inflammation on their skin, the same size as their phones. These areas of skin have become hardened after a while. In every known case, doctors have diagnosed these hardenings as dead cell tissue.

The information above has been gathered by Microshield Industries in the UK, a company that manufactures radiation protection shields for mobile phones. Perhaps they could be accused of speaking out of self-interest. But non-affiliated researchers in the world have also reported essentially the same array of symptoms – first Olle Johansson at the Karolinska Institute in Stockholm, then Bruce Hocking in Australia and Kjell Hansson Mild in Umeå, Sweden. Bruce Hocking associates these symptoms with "microwave sickness," which has been reported earlier from the Soviet Union and Eastern Europe. It was a syndrome involving the nervous systems and including fatigue, headaches, feeling "heavy headed," irritability, sleepiness, partial loss of memory, and other symptoms. People in authority in the western World waved all this aside.

The thousands of people suffering unexplained complaints when in contact with VDUs and mobile phones were given new hope in winter 2002: the Director General of WHO, The World Health Organization, stated that she, herself, was afflicted. Gro Harlem Bruntland, a former Norwegian Prime Minister, explained openly in interviews that she had symptoms from mobile phones that were switched on some meters away, and that she couldn't stand her laptop PC.

In Finland, Nokia's homeland, a doctor from the radiation-protecting agency regretted in a TV program that Gro Harlem Brundtland had "misunderstood" the causes of her symptoms. Perhaps it should be said that Gro Harlem Brundtland is a physician herself.

2

The Silicon Valley sickness worldwide

The price of our spiraling electronic development, in terms of destruction of the environment and wasted human lives, is seldom discussed. Nowhere in countries in the West has the unpleasant side of modern technology been as clearly noticeable as in Silicon Valley, the Mecca of the ITC industry in Santa Clara County, California. There one could speak of something like an asbestos catastrophe, but much more extensive, and cloaked in silence. Several decades went by before the harmful effects of asbestos were officially recognized. When it comes to chemicals and electronics, the debate hasn't even begun in earnest.

The problems that developments in Silicon Valley have left in their wake have consciously been kept quiet. When occupational illnesses in the microelectronics industry became too widespread and alarming, the Californian authorities decided to discontinue registering them. By that time they had established that the systemic poisoning rate for electronic workers was high, but even higher for the semiconductor industry, namely almost 40 per cent. Then the lid was put on. The industry also proceeded to take its own steps – production was, by and large, transferred to other countries, above all in east and southeast Asia, countries in which laws and worker protection were underdeveloped.

Corporations in the West have exported their problems. An

extremely interesting question is to what extent we in the West will have the problems returned in the form of products that have been insufficiently checked.

It was in the 1980s that I first heard about health problems in the "clean rooms" in the microelectronics industry in California. People's immune systems had been destroyed. They had pulmonary symptoms, skin rashes, joint pains, and allergies to a whole range of things. I thought it quite natural to draw parallels to what was happening in Sweden in ordinary offices.

In May 1986, when the debate in Sweden on the risks of working with VDUs had just started, the National Board of Occupational Safety and Health in Stockholm was visited by the American researcher Dr Joseph LaDou, clinical Professor of Medicine at the Division of Occupational and Environmental Medicine at the University of California School of Medicine in San Francisco. By then he had followed developments in the microelectronics industry over 20 years and seen incurable injuries develop in employees despite their having worked in the so-called clean rooms, which are completely dust-free. Even so, toxic gases, acids, and solvents were present in these clean rooms and employees complained of symptoms of toxification.

When I interviewed him in autumn 2001 Joseph LaDou confirmed that there have been far too few studies of the health problems among the employees of the microelectronics and semiconductor industry, which is currently one of the most expansive industries in the world. It is difficult to understand why work regulating and environment authorities have not reacted to what LaDou reported during his 1986 visit to Sweden. Today, the chemicals in electronics are still not an issue discussed by authorities concerned with health problems relating to electro-hypersensitivity and multiple chemical sensitivity. Admittedly, LaDou didn't talk about these symptoms among office workers when he visited Sweden, he reported on health problems in the electronics industry, but one could have expected some associations to be made by experts from public authorities.

The opinion is often heard that risks from chemicals have been eliminated in Swedish working life. But, LaDou points out, one can never eliminate chemical risks, only minimize them, and in fact chemicals can be toxic at very low levels, particularly when combined in workroom air with other chemicals. He describes the situation in clean rooms in this way:

> Clean rooms re-circulate air with dust removed, but chemical fumes and vapors are left unchanged. These chemicals react to form other chemicals that are re-circulated hour after hour. There are no protective standards for clean room re-circulated air other than a few for single chemicals – standards that are way too lenient and should not be applied in settings with combinations of chemicals such as occurs in electronics manufacture.

Silicon Valley engages in state-of-the-art manufacturing of new products. It is very competitive and fast moving. There is little time or opportunity to automate. Most activities are still manual, including the handling of large quantities of toxic chemicals, metals and gases. The same can be said for the many research and development laboratories.

Are the problems related to distinct chemicals? I asked. LaDou again:

> That is an interesting question. The industry had an explanation of why there is a 50–100 per cent increase in the incidence of spontaneous abortion in semiconductor workers. They picked out a solvent, glycol ethers (Cellosolve), and said that it was a known reproductive toxicant that was being phased out of American plants. No further questions were asked, and no further studies were conducted.
>
> There are hundreds of chemicals used by this industry. There is no compelling data to show that any single chemical causes

the problem with abortions. We are concerned about dozens of known carcinogens in the semiconductor plants. The industry blocks efforts to study the known, and suspected, health problems. For example, we are concerned with exposure to epoxy resins and epoxy hardeners, catalysts – likely explanations of the sensitizing illnesses of occupational asthma and contact dermatitis.

To a question about what radiation employees in these workplaces are exposed to, he replies:

> There is ultraviolet radiation as well as microwaves, other radio frequencies and many possible exposures to ionizing radiation as well. The use of light-sensitive chemicals in the photolithography layering of chips may cause dermatoses when combined with light radiation.
>
> Microwaves have been an exposure problem in the semiconductor industry for decades. It is difficult to study this, particularly when there are so many other agents affecting health. A comprehensive study of the health of semiconductor workers will take many years and require hundreds of thousands of workers. The US, European, and Asian industries are not going to tolerate any such study. No government is willing to sacrifice industrial development to force the companies to do so.

LaDou has seen many serious cases of illness, partly whilst practicing as an occupational physician in Sunnyvale, California. But work environments have been improved since "the early days." He mentions such things as gloves, splashguards, face shields, and safety glasses, and in recent years automatic loading techniques and more sophisticated air monitoring systems. But, he says, the risks of workplace exposure by inhalation or skin absorption have by no means been eradicated.

Joseph LaDou notes that serious occupational and environmental problems occurred from the beginning of developments in Silicon Valley, in particular with the production of semiconductor devices. But before the occupational and environmental problems were adequately addressed, the industry had migrated to many countries in the world, first to Europe and Japan, later especially to east and southeast Asia.

It is alarming, in his opinion, that the problems, to a great extent, have been moved to countries with limited environmental legislation and weak, if any, union representation. Unions were not allowed in the early high technology companies, which traditionally have demanded obedience and conformity:

> There is more semiconductor manufacturing today in Asia than in the rest of the world. The small country of Malaysia is the largest exporter of semiconductor chips in the world and the third largest producer, behind the United States and Japan. Virtually all of the industry, in Malaysia and elsewhere, is owned by US, Japanese, and European companies. The older technologies are exported to poorer countries. The chemical exposures are as bad as we used to see in the American companies thirty to forty years ago.

Malaysia also exports many of the industrial wastes to such countries as the Philippines and Thailand. But many of these countries don't have waste treatment facilities, which has resulted in illegal land filling and illicit dumping of hazardous wastes into rivers and streams. There have been reports of employee deaths in Thailand during the 1990s. Orapun Metadilogkul, a female doctor, had looked for explanations for several deaths occurring among workers at Thailand's largest industry, Seagate Technology, the US electronics giant that manufactures components for computers. In 1991, when she examined blood samples from employees, she found greatly raised levels of chemicals in them, including lead. With the help of local politicians, the company managed to tone down the findings and close the clinic where Orapun Metadilogkul worked. The politicians were anxious to keep the company in the country.

The employees who died at the Seagate plant were all in their twenties. According to fellow workers, they had earlier complained of headaches, fainting, muscle pains, and tiredness. About 200 employees had reported similar symptoms. Seagate Technology refuted all of Dr Metadilogkul's findings, among these that 36 per cent of the employees had lead levels of more than 20 micrograms per 100 milliliters of blood. Seagate maintained that the lead levels were caused by Bangkok's traffic, 20 kilometers away. Orapun Metadilogkul was able to refer to investigations that showed that only 8 per cent of the traffic police in Bangkok and 2 per cent of the average population had levels higher than 20 micrograms.

The lead levels alone were probably not the cause of the deaths. Dr. Metadilogkul also suspected other toxic substances that were used in the manufacturing. Starting in March 1994, *The Bangkok Post* published a series of articles discussing the deaths. The cause was officially given as AIDS and encephalitis, inflammation in the brain.

A very serious problem in California is that, nowadays, it is impossible to obtain exact statistical information about the occurrence of occupational illnesses in the microelectronic industry, especially the semiconductor industry. California does not publish workers' compensation data any longer, says LaDou. California long enjoyed a reputation for some of the most reliable workers' compensation data in the USA. Occupational illness data was collected by the Division of Labor Statistics and Research and were based on illness reports required of all employers in the state. It was possible to identify specific industries with high incidence rates of occupational illnesses. But, without any public discussion, California stopped publishing occupational illness data after 1991.Those who wanted information about worker health were directed to the Federal Government for data. The Bureau of Labor Statistics in the US Department of Labor compiles annual survey data from a sample of employers. In California, the Federal system samples about 20,000 employers, whereas the discontinued system compiled data from about one million employers. LaDou regrets that the accuracy of the data is much inferior to that of the statistics formerly available in California:

> The level of detail is insufficient to do targeting for preventive purposes. The definitions of injuries and illnesses are so different between the two reporting schemes that it is now impossible to compare the California experience with occupational illnesses in specific industries against the data beginning in 1992 compiled by the Federal Government.
>
> Now we're back to a reporting system for workers' compensation, which dates back to a time when no occupational illnesses, not even lead poisoning, were recognized.
>
> Only accidents are counted, occupational illnesses are not. Because no one is losing fingers making integrated circuits, at first glance the industry can seem relatively safe. But employees who are fighting against symptoms like headaches and nausea or who are losing weight because of solvent fumes are more likely to end up in the records of a personal physician than in filings with the Department of Labor. Data on occupational illnesses such as the ergonomic problems of office workers, something called carpal tunnel syndrome, and illnesses resulting from exposure to chemicals in the semiconductor industry, are not available for the past years in California. The Federal data available is not comparable for research and clinical purposes.

The industrial codes for workers' compensation offer no way to distinguish between semiconductor employees who work in the clean rooms – approximately 25 per cent of the workforce in a typical chip-making company – and the remaining 75 per cent. The circumstances of this discontinuance of traditional statistical records in California have never been explained to workers, or to the public. The reason given is that there is not sufficient staff available to keypunch the data into computers.

The data from the Federal Government indicates that there is a higher incidence of occupational illnesses in electronic workers than in the average of all manufacturing workers. There is an even higher incidence rate among semiconductor workers. According to 2001 figures from the Bureau of Labor Statistics at the US Department of Labor, the percentage of work loss injuries and illnesses involving exposure to caustic, noxious, or allergenic substances for all manufacturing industries was 2.4 for 1999. In industries producing electronic components and accessories the percentage was 6.0, whilst for companies producing semiconductors and related devices the figure was 9.7.

In workers' compensation a "work loss" case is "one excused from work by a physician for at least one full work shift". LaDou points out that these are the more serious cases. Many health complaints do not lead to being excused from work. When looking at occupational illnesses as a percentage of all reported injuries and illnesses, the picture becomes even clearer: for the manufacturing industries as a whole, the figure is 13.1 per cent for 1999, but 30.4 per cent for semiconductor and related device producers.

Thinking of all the various health problems that have arisen as people have increasingly begun to use computers, it is surprising that no parallels have been drawn with the Silicon Valley sickness. The same chemicals as those used in production are present in the electronic devices, which, on becoming heated during use, cause vaporization and/or chemical processes to start. Particles and gases in the air are just as harmful in offices with re-circulated air as they are in the clean rooms in Silicon Valley.

It is an interesting fact that figures are beginning to appear, indicating that almost a million people in California are suffering the same kind of symptoms as those reported by electro-hypersensitive people and others suffering from different syndromes without known causes. This is approximately 3.5 per cent of the population.

Synthetic chemicals, which we all have in our blood and body tissues today, were not present in the blood and tissues of people in the 1940s. After finding brominated flame-retardants in mothers' milk, a few brave researchers in Sweden have put forward the hypothesis that one important source could be all the electronics that surround people nowadays. Many peculiar sickness syndromes have appeared in the world in recent decades. The attitude of authorities is to hold them apart and give them different names instead of looking for common denominators. Then, it becomes easier to regard them as psychologically conditioned somatizations. There are already some people in Sweden who have taken a doctor's degree in Electro-hypersensitivity without looking out into the world and wondering about the correlations with other similar syndromes and new environmental factors. They have based their doctorates on an illness they don't really believe exists. And they often claim that it is only in Sweden that the phenomenon occurs.

This claim makes reading Dr. Robert O. Becker's book, *Cross Currents*, even more interesting. Becker is an American researcher whose book was published in 1990. He writes that as early as the 1980s, soon after his earlier books about biological effects of electromagnetic fields had been published, he began to receive letters from people who claimed they were hypersensitive to electricity. "I must admit that for the first years I was highly skeptical and thought it to be a question of some condition having psychological origin," he writes. But, when the flood of letters continued to increase, he realized that there must be something more tangible behind it all. He didn't devote further time to the question, but he did take the matter seriously, noting that the incidence of this syndrome continues to increase. He has no other explanation than that it might be due to the rising number of electrical devices and the sum of electromagnetic fields from various sources, "or perhaps to a change in the sensitivity of the human population".

At the same time he notes that the similarity between electro-hypersensitivity and what is known as Chronic Fatigue and

Immune Dysfunction Syndrome, CFIDS, is striking. He has also been consulted by people that have been given the latter diagnosis but who, themselves, have noticed that they feel worse in front of TVs and other electrical devices. They have not considered this sensitivity to be a major aspect of their illness, putting more importance on other factors, even though they feel better in rural areas, away from sources of electromagnetic fields.

Robert O. Becker mentions something very interesting: CFIDS is widespread in the microelectronics industry, especially in Silicon Valley. He quotes Dr. James Cone of the Department of Occupational Medicine at a San Francisco hospital, who reports that it is not a matter of patients with typical allergies but people who appear to have some kind of neurological problems or something wrong with their immune system and who consider their injuries to be work-related. Robert O. Becker comments that the characteristics of both phenomena, electro-hypersensitivity and CFIDS, involve both the central nervous and the immune systems. One conclusion given in *Cross Currents* is that if the trend continues we may be faced with extensive public health problems. Nowadays we know that public health problems have occurred; thousands of people are suffering from an additional range of syndromes with different names.

In his book Robert O. Becker describes the symptoms of a woman he calls Mary M. This description could, in every respect, refer to an electro-hypersensitive person in Sweden, or to people suffering from chronic fatigue or multiple chemical sensitivity, depending on what country they are living in and what terminology is used there.

Mary M. was a computer supervisor in a large company, perfectly healthy until she was asked to try out a new computer. The first day she had a minor headache when she went home, but the next day she felt well again. When she had sat in front of her VDU for less than an hour the headache returned. She thought that she was probably catching a cold and took an aspirin, but the headache persisted. She also felt nauseated and dizzy.

Robert O. Becker's information, though sparse, gives a lot to reflect over. Speculating on what importance chemical emissions could have had in this connection, it may be noted that a high percentage of the people in Sweden who have become sick in front of vdus have reported exactly the same thing: it occurred when they changed vdus. Logically, chemical emissions are at their highest from new equipment. Our sense of smell tells us that. Today, hopefully, most people know that they should let a new screen stand and "burn off" in a well-ventilated space for at least a week, to get rid of the smell of plastic due to the initial powerful vaporization of various chemicals. The most practical solution would be for manufacturers to burn off machines as much as possible prior to placing them in a work environment. But the customers don't know that they ought to demand that.

The following are two cases I have come across. Both are of people whose profession involved selling computers and who have taken several new machines home, letting them remain switched on over a lengthy period of time, both at their workplaces and in their homes. This is quite a common way for computer sellers to test quality. In one case, both the seller and his wife became extremely electro-hypersensitive. The wife, in addition, became so sensitive to light that she was obliged to live completely in darkness for a while. In the other case, only the wife was afflicted; she used to work in the family's electronics company where she was surrounded by devices that were running during daytime. Her husband also took home computers and kept them running there as well. There were even pcs in their bedroom.

Returning to Mary M., we can assume that she, through earlier exposure, had begun to develop sensitivity for certain chemicals emitted from computers. Now she presumably received a significant dose of the same substances from the new equipment. Perhaps this was the straw that broke the camel's back. Perhaps it should be said that Robert O. Becker doesn't mention a word about chemicals. He only tells the story as if it was a question of electromagnetic fields. What was it then that evaporated from

Mary M.'s computer screen? It is difficult to say without a chemist examining that particular VDU, but, with all probability it was at least triphenyl phosphates and brominated flame-retardants, perhaps unhardened epoxy and many other substances. It was not so strange that Mary M. felt ill.

Mary M. was also subjected to electromagnetic fields, ultraviolet radiation, and visible light from the equipment. Probably there was fluorescent lighting in the office as well. Some chemicals that were emitted from the equipment could have become toxic through contact with light. This could have been sufficient to make Mary M. hypersensitive to light. And she did, in fact, become hypersensitive to light, though not immediately. After some days at home Mary M. returned to work again, completely well. She switched the computer on and it happened again; after only a few minutes the headache, nausea, and dizziness came back. After a short time she began to feel extremely tired. She found it more and more difficult to concentrate and her sight began to deteriorate. She became completely red in the face and on parts of her throat and chest that had been exposed to light. Now she was forced to give up. When, after a week, she returned and opened the door to the office she felt as though a blast from a furnace had blown against her. There were now more VDUs in the room. She could only stay in the room for a few minutes. Then she was forced to leave. She had begun to feel very ill.

How many times have I heard this description! Hundreds of computer users in Sweden have reported the same thing. One day they come to the end of the road. They can stand it no more. In certain cases a person needs only to walk into the workplace for the symptoms to appear. Mary M. also reacted as many people do in "sick buildings" – they cannot even go into the building where they have become ill without experiencing symptoms. It may be worth noting that research into "sick building syndrome" has got nowhere, despite analyses of emissions from building materials and interior furnishing having been carried out for several decades. Could it be the case that researchers have missed the fact that very special chemicals are released from electronic devices?

Presumably some of the chemicals that were emitted from Mary M.'s screen were now present in the curtains and carpets. New amounts continued to be released into the air, as there were several VDUs in use in the room. This story ended with Mary M. staying at home. But, to her horror, she felt the same symptoms within the proximity of her TV and stereo – she even got sick simply from talking on the phone.

Many people who suffer from electro-hypersensitivity recognize this kind of progression. If we have the hypothesis that chemicals are involved, we note that TVs, stereos, and telephones have plastic cases and components that emit different substances. But, of course, all the devices used by Mary M. were not new; how could she also react to them? It is possible that she had developed such a hypersensitivity that she could not stand even tiny doses of the chemicals found in electronics, which continue to seep out even as the devices get older.

It is easy to understand how the concept of electro-hypersensitivity arose. Mary M. became ill working in front of a VDU, she subsequently became sensitive to another electronic device based on similar cathode ray tube technology, namely her TV. Later she became sensitive to even more electronic devices and sources of electromagnetic fields. Robert O. Becker writes that Mary M.'s symptoms continued to increase and that she developed something he calls allergy to sunlight. But I presume that she had become sensitive to light in general. If someone had asked her, she would most probably have said that she couldn't tolerate fluorescent light either. She may even have reacted to normal daylight – she began to go out wearing a wide-brimmed hat and sunglasses.

There are, of course, many causes of hypersensitivity to light, for example certain medicines, but it seems that something in VDUs causes this type of sensitivity. Almost all people who have been severely ill from VDUs have experienced periods when they have been more or less hypersensitive to light. Mary M. also developed symptoms that are usually referred to as multiple chemical sensitivity, or MCS. She began to react to the smell of various substances such as washing powders and perfumes. Her skin rash reappeared and she went to a dermatologist who said that everything was caused by her VDU. Some of his previous patients had shown similar symptoms. He advised her to take a rest in a rural area. She did so, and felt better. But when she returned to the city she became ill again. She never went back to her job. Mary M.'s is a tragic fate, but not an uncommon one.

It should be noted that the dermatologist clearly stated that the VDU was the cause of Mary M.'s symptoms. Swedish doctors seldom dare to do so. In the eighties consensus was reached amongst dermatologists, particularly those specializing in work-related skin complaints, about how to deal with people who claim that their suffering is related to use of computer screens. Patients are to be calmly and sympathetically told that there is no scientific proof at all that VDUs can give rise to skin problems and even less to electro-hypersensitivity.

But even though experts working for authorities explain that the problem is best understood "from a psychological point of view," it can hardly be denied that there is some kind of environment-related effect. So many people, in so many different countries, who have been telling the same story for so long cannot simply be imagining things.

At the beginning of the nineties, Associate Professor Kjell Hanson Mild of the National Institute of Working Life in Umeå, Sweden, visited the US Environmental Health Center in Dallas. It is a clinic founded by the researcher Dr. William J Rea. Here, patients were being treated for either multiple chemical sensitivity or electro-hypersensitivity, or both. Kjell Hanson Mild noted that the patients coming to the clinic had about the same symptoms as the worst afflicted by electro-hypersensitivity in Sweden. In the Dallas clinic, however, it was more usual to place emphasis on chemical hypersensitivity as the primary cause of the patients' illnesses. Mild's visit to Dallas did not lead to any measures being taken in Sweden. "This isn't my field, I'm not a chemist," was Mild's standard reply, every time I asked him about the role that chemicals could play in connection with symptoms referred to as electro-hypersensitivity in Sweden.

As patients at the Dallas clinic were given food additives, in the form of minerals, trace elements, and vitamins, one might have suspected that it would not arouse any interest in Sweden. Antioxidant therapy is something of a red rag for the National Board of Health and Welfare. There is, admittedly, a Swedish report dated 2001 about electro-hypersensitive people who had been given antioxidants. Dr Lena Hillert, who has specialized in electro-hypersensitivity, had carried out trials, without finding any positive effects. She had, however, only used Vitamin C and E together with selenium, in very low doses. Her critics, especially in Finland, were of the opinion that, in order to achieve results, one ought to measure the status of each individual with respect to micronutrients, and, based on this, try out all the substances that the person in question has deficiency in and use higher doses.

Interdisciplinary research into electro-hypersensitivity has been called for over the past twenty years. There has been none, as yet, apart from the ardent collaboration between dermatologists, psychologists, and stress therapists.

3

Epoxy, the main suspect in some occupational injuries

There are a number of similarities between the chronic symptoms of workers poisoned by epoxy, and those of office employees around the world who are suffering from apparently different illnesses, variously called electro-hypersensitivity, multiple chemical sensitivity, chronic fatigue, sick building syndrome, etc. A common mechanism and the same chemicals might be the explanation.

Over the years 1976 to 1979 76 of the 127 blue-collar workers at Svenska Fläkt in Northern Sweden, a factory which manufactured ventilation ducts and stove burners, exhibited various chronic symptoms that to a greater or lesser degree incapacitated them from working. Decomposition products from heated epoxy resin had poisoned the workers. When these chemical compounds were deposited on skin and exposed to UV light, they gave rise to chronic symptoms, mainly hypersensitivity to light. At about the same time, thousands of office workers all over the world began to have similar chronic symptoms whilst working in front of VDUs. There were isolated cases, but also clusters of many afflicted in some offices. Experts didn't draw any parallels.

What could the workers at Svenska Fläkt and the VDU-users in offices have in common? There are many similarities. It is obviously a question of almost identical symptoms. The parallel is made even more interesting by the fact that there is epoxy in various computer components. The possibility that lies near to hand is that other of the chemicals used in electronics react in a similar manner as epoxy, when heated and exposed to light or perhaps other electromagnetic radiation. If they do so we have a common mechanism in both cases. The argument against the people who have become sick in front of computer screens has always been that there is no mechanism that could explain the connection between their symptoms and the electromagnetic fields from computers. People have, in this context, only discussed electromagnetic fields, not the combination effects of radiation and chemicals.

At first the workers at Svenska Fläkt complained about stinging and burning sensations in their faces. Initially the doctors were unable to see any skin changes. Subsequently some of the workers showed gradual reddening, others edema and eczema-like rashes. Nothing was observed around eyes, or under the nose or chin. Most had bloodshot eyes and other eye complaints such as burning or a gritty feeling, irritation, dryness, and increased tear production.

Forty-nine of the workers afflicted got persistent problems, including hypersensitivity to light, mainly sunlight, but also artificial light from unshielded fluorescent lighting and halogen lamps. Many complained that they could no longer watch TV or spend time in public places with fluorescent lighting. Some of them could no longer go out fishing or doing other kinds of outdoor activities that they were used to, because they couldn't tolerate sunshine, especially during the first summer after they had become sick.

Examination revealed that they were sensitive to ultraviolet radiation, UV-A as well as UV-B, in other words both long- and short-wave UV radiation. They also reacted to visible light, which seemed to aggravate their symptoms. Obviously it was a question of some form of photo-allergic or phototoxic reaction, in other words an effect of a combination of chemical substances and light.

Those who are severely affected after using VDUs also exhibit sensitivity to light, often ordinary visible light. When the patients from Svenska Fläkt came to the occupational dermatology department in the University Hospital in Umeå, the staff turned off the fluorescent lighting for them. The same consideration was given, only a few years later, to another category of patients, those affected by VDUs. The Svenska Fläkt victims had also problems with heat, cold, and wind. Their symptoms were worsened by "dust," as well as by substances in products such as perfumes, paints, and petrol. Obviously their skin was damaged and very sensitive to everything.

In the early stages no one understood what could have caused the employees to become so sensitive. All the affected people had worked in the same workshop. Some office staff, who paid regular visits to the workshop, developed similar symptoms. After a while the cause of the chronic symptoms that so many of those in the Svenska Fläkt epidemic developed was understood. The factory had a paint shop in which burner covers were coated using electrostatic powder sprays. Epoxy from the paint shop was sucked into the factory's ventilation, the polluted air being heated in the system and recycled through the factory. Traces of paint powder were found in the heater and throughout the entire ventilation system.

An expert group, which included doctors and occupational inspectors, investigated the case. By experimenting they concluded that when the epoxy had been exposed to heat, the bonding agent in the paint had decomposed and been released into the air. The decomposition products were phototoxic, that is they became poisonous when exposed to light. People who got these substances on their skin became sensitive to light and got various other symptoms, too. When the chain of events was reconstructed, it was found that the symptoms were at a maximum when all the machines in the factory workshop were running and all the strip lighting in the ceilings was switched on.

Per-Anders Zingmark is one of the occupational inspectors who had been called to Svenska Fläkt. I interviewed him some years ago about the events which most people have forgotten today, except for the afflicted themselves. He said that "a whole forest" of chemical combinations was formed so it was impossible to make a ruling about exactly which of them were the active ingredients. "On the other hand we could demonstrate by experiments what happened when the paint was heated. Patch tests also revealed that the people affected reacted to the decomposition products."

He recalled that the workers complained they felt as though they had lain in the sun and become sunburned. Thousands of vdu-users around the world have reported the same thing for years, without doctors daring to take them seriously. Per-Anders Zingmark was not prepared to draw any parallels to electro-hypersensitive people when I asked him, perhaps because he had never been in contact with vdu-injured people and didn't know much about that problem. In his opinion you need to differentiate between what initiates the symptoms in the first place and what protracts them later: "The body doesn't have so many ways of reacting. Even though symptoms appear to be similar, the cause may not be exactly the same."

But the feeling of intense sunburn reported by vdu-users has usually been the starting point of incapacity to continue working with screens. Many have tried to stand the feeling of heat and smarting pain as long as possible but, in the end, have been forced to give up and are chronically ill today.

When the Svenska Fläkt factory had been sanitized, no new cases occurred there. But, in 1983 a similar case was reported at another Swedish company where epoxy paints had also been used. A man had become chronically hypersensitive to light. The National Swedish Defense Establishment, FOA, ran tests, confirming that when heated both the paint and the bonding agent used formed substances that give rise to eczema if they come into contact with skin, which is simultaneously exposed to light.

Problems caused by epoxy are more common than I knew before I started to seek the truth behind the VDU-sickness. People who, in the industry, have worked with printed circuit cards often have chronic symptoms in the skin and are also more or less sensitive to light. The mechanism that gives sensitivity to light is nothing new. Certain medicines, for example, provoke such sensitivity. Some plants can also do so. If sap from wild giant chervil is rubbed on the skin and this is exposed to sunlight, the result is skin burns. It is also known that taking certain antibiotics before lying in the sun or in a solarium may cause light sensitivity. Thus certain chemicals can produce new, unexpected biological effects through exposure to light.

This combination effect is used in the so-called PUVA treatment for psoriasis. PUVA is an abbreviation for psoralen-ultra-violet activity. Psoralen is a substance that makes skin sensitive to light. There are very precise regulations concerning how many seconds patients may be exposed to light during PUVA-treatment. Despite that, it has been reported that there is a 30 per cent increase in cancer risk for patients who have taken the treatment.

Associate Professor Berndt Stenberg at University Hospital in Umeå, where the Svenska Fläkt cases had been treated, took part in the following up of their symptoms. His work included editing a booklet entitled *Fläkt sickness – ten years on*, published in 1990 by the Institute for Occupational Safety and Health. It showed that many of the workers still had symptoms, including stinging and burning sensations in facial skin. They also had problem with their eyes, especially under fluorescent lighting. They could not tolerate car fans, heat, or cold. They reacted to such things as hairsprays and solvents and the mere smell of chemicals in general, symptoms also very common in the syndrome called multiple chemical sensitivity.

During the follow-up it was established that, despite treatment with cortisone ointment and suchlike, some of the workers had increased symptoms. But practically everyone was satisfied with the support they had received from authorities regarding disability pensions, medical tests, rehabilitation, and other things. The Social Insurance Office had seen to it that everyone had got his/her occupation injuries and benefits settled. The VDU-injured have never experienced support of that kind. Doctors and authorities have laughed at them.

In the report written in the follow-up, it was emphasized that the symptoms of the Svenska Fläkt workers were subjective; they were no longer visible. This had created some lack of understanding among people close to these afflicted. I have interviewed some of the Svenska Fläkt workers. Egil Lindström is one of them. He was 68 years old when I spoke with him. Then he had not worked since 1978, owing to his injuries. He still had symptoms under fluorescent lighting. "If I go into a department store, my face starts burning after ten minutes. The symptoms are still there in the evening and the following day. Nowadays I can watch TV. I couldn't before. I couldn't tolerate the fan in my car and the scent of perfume was unbearable."

Nobody wanted to say exactly which substance in the epoxy resin caused the symptoms occurring in Svenska Fläkt's employees, at least not officially. The question was sensitive; rumor said the chemical suppliers' lawyers exerted great pressure on the group of experts who investigated the case. The product must not be condemned. Despite interviews with many of those involved in the Svenska Fläkt case it was not until the 1990s that I found someone who was prepared to express an opinion in public about the substance that caused the chronic suffering for so many of the factory workers at Svenska Fläkt. This person was Per Hedemalm, MSc.

Per Hedemalm was formerly employed by the Swedish Institute of Production Engineering Research in Gothenburg. Nowadays he is active as an environmental consultant. He is one of the foremost experts in the world when it comes to chemicals in electronics and has systematically surveyed the various substances in a report commissioned by the Nordic Council of Ministers, entitled *Waste from electrical and electronic products, a survey of the contents of materials and hazardous substances in electric and electronic products*, published in 1995. It was the only comprehensive survey of materials and harmful substances in these products in existence. But, the report had remained at the Council's office in Copenhagen, Denmark, without action being taken. It was impossible to obtain even a single copy of it in Sweden. The media completely missed it, even though it had been specifically produced to give the Nordic authorities knowledge in the field prior to new legislation on manufacturers' responsibility for products of this type. It was also intended to be a basis for debate on this ticking environmental bomb.

Per Hedemalm is convinced that the villain in the act at Svenska Fläkt was Bisphenol-A. He has never been directly involved in the case, but has read the information available and found three cases of workplace injuries similar to Svenska Fläkt documented in the scientific literature. One of these was described in a dermatological journal, *Archives of Dermatology*, vol. 115, November 1979, the same period as the workers in Sweden were studied at the Umeå University Hospital.

Two American researchers, Herbert Allen and Kays Kaidbey, describe in the journal an occupational injury, which concerned eight employees at a gas and electricity firm. They got reddened skins, edemas (accumulation of water in the skin), enlarged blood vessels, and rashes two weeks after being exposed to fumes from heated epoxy whilst they were laying cables.

The worst symptoms disappeared after treatment. But

suddenly, two months later, all eight got skin complaints again after a short while in sunlight, outdoors or through windows. Really small doses of UV-A gave strong reactions in seven of the eight men. They complained that they felt burning and pricking sensations in the same areas of skin that had previously been exposed to epoxy fumes. They could no longer put up with light on these parts of their bodies. Two of them even got symptoms from fluorescent lighting.

The men went through skin tests and it was found that all of them reacted to Bishenol-A, an ingredient in epoxy. No medicine had beneficial effects. The only thing that helped was to keep out of sunlight and away from other sources of light. Some of them were sensitive to even the smallest ray of light. As late as a year after the exposure they had to stay indoors during daytime. Almost all of them continued to be chronically sensitive to light.

Allen and Kaidbey drew the conclusion that the men's hypersensitivity to light was, with all probability, triggered by Bisphenol-A and other substances arising from the decomposition of epoxy or closely related chemicals. The researchers called attention to the fact that the time between exposure to epoxy and the first signs of becoming sensitized to light may be long. Even when hypersensitivity has developed the time between exposure to light and symptoms arising may be as long as up to a month. They thought that the reason why hypersensitivity to light became permanent was that the substances producing it remained in the skin. They also thought UV radiation determined how deeply these substances could penetrate into the skin. The theory that the substances remain in the skin explains why the men didn't react on parts of their bodies that hadn't been exposed to epoxy when, later, they were given skin tests using UV-A and UV-B, the researchers concluded.

There has not been much discussion about reactions of this kind. During the 1960s an epidemic of photo-allergies broke out in the USA, caused by a certain type of soap that contained chlorinated phenols. The soap was quickly taken off the market.

No real debate on substances that could cause this type of reaction took place after that. However, Allen and Kaidbey write that at the end of the 1970s reports began to appear about a number of substances that could cause hypersensitivity to light.

It may be added that at this time more and more people in the West began sitting in front of computers day after day, surrounded by an increasing number of other electronic devices, all protected by flame-retardants containing chlorinated and brominated phenols, also a wide range of other substances that had never been tested with respect to health risks.

When it concerns VDUs and other electronic equipment it's not a question of soaps that can be taken off the market. Now we have to do with the whole world economy and a mighty chemical industry, not to mention the electronics industry.

What is epoxy? The raw materials of various groups of epoxy, called resins, are Bisphenol-A (BPA) and epichlorhydrine. Bisphenol-A is a phenol combination and epichlorhydrine is an unstable liquid, primarily used in the production of epoxy resins. It is harmful if inhaled or in contact with skin. The finished, hardened epoxy resin is a mixture of various long-chained molecules in which only small residues of free, unhardened Bisphenol-A should be present. But there is still enough left in cold hardened products to cause allergic reactions. According to available information, epoxy resin causes allergy principally through its content of diglycolic acid in Bisphenol-A.

Animal tests and laboratory experiments show that Bisphenol-A is broken down by UV light. Per Hedemalm also says that it is proven that Bisphenol-A can provoke light sensitivity in mice. "It must be considered proven that Bisphenol-A can give rise to photo-allergies, i.e. that it is a photosensitizing substance," he says. "I have, however, not seen any proof that it is phototoxic, in other words that it has a poisonous effect, even though you could have a strong suspicion after reading about the symptoms arising in people who have become photosensitized through Bisphenol-A."

There are pollutants in Bisphenol-A, so other substances may be formed during decomposition, Per Hedemalm says. He also mentions that, when heated, Bisphenol- A may be broken down to indane, which because of its chemical structure is regarded as being capable of penetrating into inner body organs.

> It is soluble in fats and thus, can be stored in the body, for example in nerves that are rich in fats. Indane contains both phenol and propene, both of which are highly allergenic; they can easily attach themselves to cells in the body.
>
> It isn't unthinkable that indane may give rise to reactions that result in light sensitivity. As far as I know amounts of indane present in electronics have never been measured. As it is reactive it is certainly not easy to detect. It is also probable that the amounts present depend on which fluxing agent has been used during soldering.

Per Hedemalm has pondered over the mysterious VDU sickness that no one seems to have found an explanation for, and doesn't hesitate to compare it with the Svenska Fläkt accident. He goes one step further: "Brominated Bisphenol-A, used as flame retardant for example in computer screens, can be expected to have properties that may cause hypersensitivity to light to an even greater extent than Bisphenol-A," he says. Thus there could be a clear link between the Svenska Fläkt cases and the VDU-injured. Printed circuit cards used in VDUs and electronic devices in general are almost all based on epoxy, where the Bisphenol-A components are replaced by the flame retardant, Tetrabromobisphenol-A (TBBPA).

During normal use, epoxies in computer equipment may be heated up to 125 degrees Celsius. Small amounts of free TBBPA may be emitted and attracted to charged particles of dust which then irritate the skin and eyes, says Per Hedemalm.

It isn't any problem to detect TBBPA from electronic equipment, that's already been done in a number of experiments. But one ought to go a step further and show that in very low concentrations these substances, together with electromagnetic radiation within the visible light spectrum may give rise to hypersensitivity reactions. It is known, and documented, that chlorinated phenols do cause hypersensitivity to UV light.

It will probably be necessary to carry out animal experiments to find out if Per Hedemalm's hypothesis is correct. But it should not require extensive, nor expensive, research. The problem is to find a researcher who understands the context.

In 1991 Per Hedemalm, his colleague Per Carlsson at the Institute of Production Engineering Research, and Professor Leif Holmlid at Chalmers University of Technology in Gothenburg applied to the Work Environment Fund for funding to investigate the decomposition of flame-retardants from printed circuit boards in VDUs and their possible reaction with ozone.

They referred to the fact that IBM, in 1990, had shown that measurable amounts of phenols, substances that are known to cause allergies, hypersensitivity, and also light sensitivity, could be found in the air around the computer screens. Phenol compounds that give the characteristic smell from new equipment are emitted from different components. In their funding application, they wrote: "A possibility that hitherto has not been paid attention to is that ozone and decomposition products from flame-retardants may be able to react with each other, for example forming free radicals or other products that may strengthen the allergenic effects that these substances possess." Ozone is formed in copying machines and laser printers. It is a highly reactive substance that contributes to various other reactions "in most unpredictable ways," as Per Hedemalm puts it.

In a comment on the application, the National Board of Occupational Safety and Health wrote: "Unfounded statements on the occurrence of chemical substances together with an uncritical reference to IBM's study make the reasoning with respect to work environmental risks appear to be poorly substantiated and rather speculative."

But the Gothenburg researchers didn't allow themselves to be satisfied with the rejection. They didn't make any further formal applications for funding, but they sounded out the terrain and put forward their arguments in other ways. They noticed that it was like beating their heads against a brick wall, as Per Hedemalm recalls: "It was as though the work environment aspects didn't concern anyone. No one took overall responsibility for the environmental effects of products."

Nevertheless, people at the National Board of Occupational Safety and Health perhaps felt that something ought to be done following IBM's revelation, so they convened a conference to discuss the question of chemicals in the VDUs. Two doctors, Mats Berg, known from the TCO-questionnaire mentioned in Chapter 1, and Carola Lidén explained that no one had found proof of VDUs causing any skin complaints whatsoever. Thus there was no need to start research on chemical risks connected with using VDUs. At this time the number of people suffering from the effects of VDUs in Sweden alone was in its thousands.

By 1997 Per Hedemalm and his colleagues were once again ready to commence extensive research into these matters. They discussed the question with SIF, the Swedish Union of Clerical and Technical Employees in Industry, but the union was not prepared to provide the funding necessary to carry out the research, so nothing came of their proposal. "We couldn't start such a large project without the backing of an organization," says Per Hedemalm.

Nowadays he has other irons in the fire. Someone else is needed to take up the issues he raised and find out if he was right. But who?

4

An unprescribed "treatment"

A combination of light and chemicals is used in the so-called PUVA-treatment for psoriasis. Some types of changes in the skin, side effects of this treatment, are similar to skin changes in VDU-users. Are we all involuntarily PUVA treated in front of our computer screens? Not with the same chemical, but with something similar, reacting in the same way. The mechanism could perhaps be the same.

This line of inquiry has never been investigated. However, some years after the outbreak of the epidemic at Svenska Fläkt, described in Chapter 3, the skin specialist Berndt Stenberg at Umeå University Hospital had a new group of patients who showed almost identical symptoms – this time office workers who had become ill after using VDUs.

Among the first of these new patients were nine, of a total of fourteen, employees at Bowater, a wood processing plant in Umeå. They started to have severe skin complaints shortly after IBM screens had been installed in their office. All of them had worked in the company for a long time without having any skin problems. With the IBM computers everything changed. Their symptoms were the same as those reported by VDU operators around the world.

One important factor in this context is worth noting: at the time, there was no debate in Sweden about skin problems related to the use of computers. So, the Bowater employees couldn't have been influenced by the Swedish media debate about VDUs and skin problems that started two to three years later, in autumn 1985. This has been completely overlooked by those who are convinced that it was journalists and unions, who, by exaggerating a few isolated cases, created an epidemic of skin complaints related to VDUs. As I was involved, I can assure anyone that this was not the case. When the debate began in the media many people reported that they had suffered from these problems already, from the 1970s, without doctors taking them seriously.

But, of course, when the debate had started there could have been individuals who tried to find "explanations" for problems of different kinds in their lives by referring to VDUs. But I have the impression that they were very few. They are not interesting in this context, when we have a situation in which people with severe and chronic symptoms don't get help. Too many try to escape the questions: What are the causes of these real occupational injuries and what can be done for the victims?

Some of those in the Bowater office in Umeå had very visible skin changes in the form of reddening and swellings. Berndt Stenberg presented photos of these at the first international VDU conference held in 1986, in Stockholm. He had touched upon the thought that it could be a question of the same mechanism in the Svenska Fläkt factory and in Bowater. He had run tests for substances known as terpenes from the timber handled at the Bowater workplace, but without reaching any conclusions. He had also done a little experiment with emissions from VDUs, but he couldn't find any sensitizing substances.

At the time there was no database relating to chemicals that are found in VDUs, even less of investigations on the extent to which chemicals are emitted into the air around electrical and electronic devices. When, in 1990, IBM admitted that different substances could be measured in the air around their VDUs it was said that the amounts in question in office environments were "below prescribed limits" and thereby harmless. This is an argument both common and misleading. Recent research into certain chemicals shows that people who have become hypersensitive react to levels well below prescribed limits, if such limits exist. In addition, the limits prescribed are the result of numerous different compromises and often lacking in relevance. It even appears possible that lower doses of certain chemicals give rise to stronger reactions than higher ones.

Another aspect is that very little is known about the effects of different combinations of chemicals when they interact with one another or are in combination with electromagnetic radiation, for example in the form of UV light. Above all, the argument that it is a matter of low levels lacks relevance nowadays, as we know that certain flame-retardants, for example, are soluble in fats and accumulate in the body. Thus, over time, it may become a question of relatively high levels.

At the beginning of the 1980s when the Bowater cases were treated in Umeå, both chlorinated and brominated flame-retardants were used in the plastic cases of electronic devices. Both of these types of flame-retardants accumulate in fatty tissues. On some of the photos of patients that Berndt Stenberg presented at the 1986 Conference in Stockholm one could see such remarkable skin changes that one might have asked if it could have been a question of some form of chloracne.

Berndt Stenberg observed the similarity between the Svenska Fläkt cases and the Bowater employees, for example the light sensitivity. But he also thought that there was a difference: the former reacted clearly to ultraviolet light and were "genuinely" sensitive to light, as he put it. He tested the VDU cases, too, but could not observe that they reacted to either UV-B or UV-A in general. On the other hand, they seemed to be sensitive to visible light, which he found surprising.

Recalling the experience of the American researchers Allen and Kaidbey, when they studied the workers injured by epoxy, it is reasonable to note that the workers were sensitive to light only on the surfaces which had been exposed to both light and chemicals. It can be difficult to get to know the whole truth about VDU-patients if one carries out light tests on other body parts than those affected by chemicals and light. The VDU-operators who have been carefully studied under a microscope, and they are few, have skin injuries mainly on the parts of their bodies that have been exposed to light. Furthermore, according to the literature about them, the Svenska Fläkt workers seemed to have their symptoms aggravated by visible light, too. Details perhaps, but details often lead to the truth.

Concerning hypersensitivity to light there seems to be a whole range of variations and inter-reactions. No one is able to talk about them with any great degree of certainty. I suspect that those suffering VDU-related injuries would have been able to contribute to increased knowledge about light sensitivity if the doctors had only examined them carefully and listened to them. But only a few in this group of patients have been given the type of examination and attention required. Perhaps not one among them has reached a doctor specialized on light sensitivity before they have been referred to a psychologist.

✖

In autumn 2001, Berndt Stenberg took part in a workshop in Stockholm about electro-hypersensitivity where the technician Per Hedemalm (see Chapter 3), gave a presentation of his hypothesis that VDU-sickness could, quite simply, be caused by interactive processes between chemicals and light.

This was the first time the skin specialist Berndt Stenberg and the engineer Per Hedemalm met to discuss if electro-hypersensitivity could have something to do with already known forms of chronic actinic (coming from radiation) light sensitivity. It was a somewhat dramatic meeting.

Berndt Stenberg complained that Per Hedemalm didn't make a clear distinction between symptoms caused by photo-allergic and phototoxic mechanisms. It became a rather heated discussion about these dermatological definitions, rather than a discussion of which chemicals are present in VDUs and other electronic devices and what health effects these might have.

For a layman it's probably not so important to know exactly what the terms photo-allergic and phototoxic mean; in both cases chemicals and radiation of some kind are necessary. What happens in photo-allergies is that a substance, which in itself doesn't cause an allergy, absorbs energy from light and this energy causes molecules to alter their structures so that the substance becomes allergenic. In phototoxic reactions the question is about an already toxic substance absorbing UV light.

For us in the audience it was too much of a discussion about details. Once again we realized that there will not be any study on this issue in the future. Apparently the doctors didn't like it that a technician, who hasn't done any scientific study especially about electro-hypersensitivity, presented a hypothesis that might show that there were factors the doctors had missed.

In his doctoral thesis, *Office Illness*, from 1994, Berndt Stenberg had discussed indoor air problems in offices and mentioned also the facial skin problems experienced by VDU-users. His conclusion was that personal and psychosocial factors as well as indoor air quality factors and physical factors associated with electromagnetic conditions are risk factors for skin symptoms in VDU-users. But he didn't discuss the mechanism which can create light sensitivity.

In an interview I had with Berndt Stenberg after the workshop in 2001, he admitted that it was an interesting idea that sick VDU operators are similar to those suffering from chronic light sensitivity as they "undoubtedly react to visible light".

> But sensitivity to visible light is only scientifically described following photo-allergic reactions, not after phototoxic ones. But I'm not saying that this isn't possible, just that it hasn't been described.
>
> The crux of the matter is that the pattern of symptoms in

the VDU cases is closer to phototoxic reactions, which are not known to cause chronic light sensitivity. That's what makes things so contradictory, but perhaps it's a question of a variation in which visible light is involved.

Twenty years after having both the Svenska Fläkt cases and the Bowater ones "on the table" at the University Hospital in Umeå, Berndt Stenberg makes the reflection that the VDU cases' sensitivity to visible light is something that, perhaps, should have been given more consideration: "Of course, it was an interesting clue. But we had no equipment to examine the visible spectrum so we were never able to follow this up."

Berndt Stenberg is, however, skeptical concerning the suggestion that so much UV light should be emitted from computer screens that it would be of importance. Per Hedemalm, on the other hand, thinks that the quantity is sufficient for those who already have been exposed to chemicals and become sensitized:

There are measurements showing that computer screens can emit more UV radiation than levels known to cause hypersensitive people to have symptoms. From literature it can be seen that the lowest level at which previously hypersensitized people have had symptoms is less than 1 mJoule per square meter.

When screens are developed, producers certainly try to ensure that the level of UV radiation is at such a low level that it should not be able to have any effects, but it's questionable whether or not every manufacturer really has taken measurements.

Per Hedemalm points out that people's sensitivity to UV light often extends to the visible spectrum. No one, on the other hand, has investigated if the sensitivity can extend into microwave frequencies, for example, he says. We do know, however, that certain chemical reactions can be accelerated by microwaves. When the microwaves create a heating effect it can speed up the rate of reactions. "Some chemical reactions take place much more quickly in microwave fields, something that industry plans to utilize."

There are many forms of chronic actinic light sensitivity that Per Hedemalm speaks about. Usually they are classified as idiopathic, that is, arising for no known reason. The illnesses occurring here are regarded as belonging to the most serious forms of light sensitivity. It is known that they are provoked by ultra-violet and visible light. "But how can one explain that VDU-injured people and people who have developed sensitivity to mobile phones react to electromagnetic fields through walls and to hidden mobile phones," I asked Per Hedemalm after the debate in Stockholm. He had an answer:

> UV light is, of course, a kind of electromagnetic radiation. Since bisphenols can be broken down by UV light, it isn't so far-fetched to think that they may be broken down by other types of electromagnetic radiation as well. There is a link between phenols and hypersensitivity to UV and visible light. The step from there to hypersensitivity to other types of electromagnetic radiation is not so long. For example, water molecules are broken down in electromagnetic fields of about 2.4 gigahertz as a result of a resonance phenomenon. I don't know if the resonance frequencies of, for example, Bisphenol-A have been measured. But UV light goes quite a way towards an explanation if it is the case that chronic actinic light sensitivity can be triggered by bisphenols from computer equipment.

"And how do you get all these substances on your skin?" I asked. Per Hedemalm says that measurements carried out in the Swedish Institute of Production Engineering Research show that substances called photo-initiators are easily emitted from the solder mask, the thin surface layer, made of epoxy, in the printed circuit boards. These substances make the epoxy chemically active on exposure to light, for instance fluorescent light. "The decomposition products can, for example, attach themselves to carbon and soot particles, which easily become electrically charged and then deposit themselves on the computer operator's skin."

5

Light sensitivity

Skin specialists have overlooked one of the most common symptoms in connection with VDU-sickness, namely light sensitivity. In severe cases the afflicted are forced to live in total darkness. There is a scientific report about a woman who felt ill when in front of her VDU and, for a time, suffered a total loss of melanocytes, the cells that form pigment in skin. In other words, her skin had no protection against light. Her case is not unique. "More suitable for publication in psychiatric journals" was the reason given by a considerable number of dermatological journals in different countries when they refused to publish an article on light sensitivity, suffered in the form of severe skin problems by this woman. In April 1999 the article was finally published, without hesitation, in the *Journal of Australian College of Nutritional and Environmental Medicine*. The authors were Swedes: Associate Professor Olle Johansson and Dr. Peng-Yue Liu at the Karolinska Institute, Stockholm, Dr. Anders Enhamre, one of the Mörby team of doctors, Stockholm-Danderyd, and Professor Lennart Wetterberg of the psychiatry clinic at St. Göran's Hospital, Stockholm. The latter is well known for his light treatment of depression.

Why then was the article seen to be so controversial in Europe? It was probably the link to "VDU sickness," which was clearly indicated in the title: A Case of Extreme and General Cutaneous Light Sensitivity in Combination with so called "Screen Dermatitis" and "Electrosensitivity" – a Successful Rehabilitation after Vitamin A Treatment – a case report. The article was associated with two phenomena that have not yet been scientifically accepted – screen dermatitis (skin inflammation related to use of VDUs) and electrohypersensitivity. The attitude to all this has been fairly unanimous at international scientific conferences on electromagnetic fields: such things must be regarded as mental disturbances – the question of health hazards from electromagnetic fields, such as cancer, have in themselves been sufficiently controversial. To begin discussing acute symptoms is just too much...

There are people with this kind of acute symptom in many countries, but they find it difficult to make themselves heard. Unlike employees in Sweden, they have not had support forthcoming from unions. Thus, in most countries doctors and researchers are not aware that there is a real problem. Those who want to can afford to make fun of the Swedish debate.

An episode from a conference on VDU-related health hazards, held in Germany in the 1990s, can be used to illustrate the situation. Associated Professor Yngve Hamnerius from Chalmers University of Technology, Gothenburg, gave an account of a provocation experiment that he had carried out on electrosensitive subjects. One of the conference delegates found it appropriate to explain that these types of symptoms were regarded as an expression of schizophrenia in other parts of Europe. "We, too, have that type of patient in Sweden, but it's not them I'm discussing now," was Yngve Hamnerius' quick and pointed reply. Though he was unable to prove that it was electromagnetic fields that gave rise to these acute symptoms, he knew that those afflicted were mentally normal, highly educated technicians being over-represented. Since the 1980s he had visited numerous places of work and made measurements in environments in which people had real problems.

With the publication of the above-mentioned article some Swedish researchers made a new kind of contribution to the debate. They shed light on one of the most overlooked manifestations of this complex of symptoms that has been called electro-hypersensitivity. In the article published in Australia the authors describe how a 47-year-old woman had developed the typical symptoms associated with using VDUs in the years following 1988. Periodically she felt better but always had relapses. The woman, who had been working in an office with many computers, became sensitive to light in the early stages and experienced a period in which she was forced to stay indoors for several months. She recovered after taking concentrated doses of beta-carotene. In June 1994 she was afflicted by extreme sensitivity to light. After exposing her back to sunlight through a window for half-an-hour she suddenly developed a rapidly developing total sensitivity to all kinds of light. She complained of an intense burning sensation in her skin and, later on, in tissues at a greater depth. The skin, however, appeared to be normal. Her body temperature was also normal. She covered herself with thick dark clothes and stayed indoors in almost complete darkness, leaving her house only for short walks in the evening when the sun had set and keeping to the shade of woodland paths. In the beginning she felt that the symptoms had developed mostly in her face, hands, feet, and thighs. Later her whole body reacted. This time not even beta-carotene helped. She didn't feel that her eyes were sensitive to normal light, but if she was exposed to very strong light she became light sensitized over her whole body. No visible changes were seen in her skin. In January 1995 she was prescribed large doses of vitamin A, to begin with daily for a three-month period, thereafter in two-week periods. She was also advised to exercise. By summer 1996 she could expose herself to indirect sunlight if she kept in the shade and only went out in the late afternoons. But it was not until 1998 that she reported that her sensitivity to light had almost completely disappeared. On the other hand she could not watch TV, talk on the phone for long periods or stand beside the electric oven in her home.

During the worst period, 1994, and also in June 1996, Olle Johansson and his colleagues took skin biopsies from her right thigh, just above the knee, and studied them by means of immunofluorescence microscopy. For control purposes similar biopsies were taken from healthy volunteers. The researchers write that to their "great surprise" they found that the numbers of two types of dendritic cells were dramatically reduced in the first biopsy, especially in the epidermis, i.e. the top layer of skin. The cells were both fewer and thinner than normal. In the biopsy taken when she had recovered, the picture under the microscope was normal. Whilst in her most light sensitive period the woman had lost her melanocytes – the cells that form pigment in skin. In other words, her skin had no protection against light.

The authors point out that the only factors that have been reported earlier as giving rise to similar damage to the skin's immune system are UV light, x-rays, and ionizing radiation, i.e. radioactivity. They also discuss whether or not vitamin A, which is essential to human sight, may also affect the cellular system of the skin. They do not rule out chemicals as a basic cause of the woman's cellular changes, but point out that the cause of screen dermatitis is not known. The only thing they can do is to describe the woman's cell changes, having noted that she is sensitive to electromagnetic radiation, including light.

With respect to those afflicted with acute symptoms follow-ing VDU work, these cell changes are more concrete findings than other researchers have hitherto produced. But those in Sweden who have "preferential right of interpretation" when it comes to this group of patients have found silence to be their best argu-ment.

When reading the article a reflection that may be made is that the woman's "avoidance behavior" is fully adequate. Instinctively, she did what she had to do to protect herself against light. The article also awakens many recollections of how people have been treated over the years. I remember a case of a young female bank clerk who had the same symptoms as those given for the woman covered in the scientific analysis. However, this clerk was treated by a doctor, who, when her symptoms were most acute, cheerfully advised her to go out in the sunlight. Fortunately, she didn't follow the advice. She happened to live in Småland, a rural area, and withdrew to an isolated cottage where she thought she felt better and was able to go out into the woods during cloudy weather. Her case caused a professor to talk about how unreasonable it was to "take people who hide behind curtains in Småland seriously".

I interviewed this young woman in the 1980s. We sat in her little eighteenth-century cottage with the curtains drawn. The whole situation had an air of hopelessness about it. Until recently she had been a capable, well-liked bank clerk in a town some miles away, where she still had a modern apartment. But now her whole life was devastated, she had been forced to give up all her dreams of a career.

Now, when I read what I wrote about her, I see that I had noted that she was sensitive to chemicals and certain foods. Some work had been carried out on the old cottage and she had reacted strongly to some materials used, including paints. At he time I had no idea of the light–chemical mechanisms that can give rise to light sensitivity. If any of the doctors that I interviewed had told me that such mechanisms had been known for decades, perhaps I would have thought of asking questions about the chemicals emitted from the various VDUs this young woman had worked with.

When her first symptoms appeared her face swelled up and became stiff as if she had been given a local anesthetic. She had been surrounded by six computer screens, two color TVs, a copying machine, ten electric typewriters and numerous strip lights. In her immediate surroundings was a Grundig Super Color-terminal. Some years later a technician raised the alarm about the possibility of there being as many as 20–30 kg of brominated flame-retardants in the plastic cases and components of devices in use in an average-sized office. This didn't receive much notice from the authorities concerned with occupational health or from doctors. They continued to talk about the psychosocial causes of the mysterious symptoms among office workers. Nowadays flame-retardants are discussed in Sweden but no authority has, as yet, associated them with people who have become ill whilst working in office environments.

Eija Salmela, another woman, who lives in Räyrinki, Finland, has experienced the same total sensitivity to light as the woman described in the scientific article published in Australia. But no skin biopsies were taken from her. Not even when she was going through her most sensitive period was it considered worth the effort of studying her more deeply. It is a pity that no researcher was at hand. If that had been the case, judging from the information available, it is likely that an equally interesting scientific article on light sensitivity following working with vdus could have been written in Finland. One might add that this would have been useful for those afflicted with similar symptoms in Finland. Finnish doctors are not willing to treat any kind of symptom that patients believe to have been caused by using vdus. They just say this is "the Swedish sickness".

However, Eija Salmela has kept her own records of symptoms, after being advised to do so by a Swedish company doctor that she was in contact with earlier. Having met her, I have had the opportunity of reading these notes. She is one of the thousands of young Finnish people who moved to work in Sweden after being educated in Finland. In her case this was tragic as neither country takes responsibility for her situation today.

She became sick when working at the Swedish State Power Corporation in Stockholm, where she commenced employment in 1985. In spring 1990 she began to feel hotness on her right cheekbone, two weeks after starting to use a Swedish manufactured Facit vdu on her desk. The screen had been in use for half a year. The employer quickly saw to it that a filter was installed and properly earthed.

The problem didn't recur until September 1991. Her department was moved up one floor into an open-plan office. In connection with the move, earthing Eija Salmela's screen was overlooked. Shortly thereafter she began to have problems again. Towards evening she began to feel as though she had been sunbathing for too long. Her skin became sensitive to touch. Her cosmetologist pointed out that she had patches of redness on her cheeks and chin. When her cheeks began to smart she realized that the trouble was caused by her VDU. People around her were sympathetic, and some measures were taken in her work environment so that she didn't have so many devices that produced electromagnetic fields around her. She tried to persevere for three months. "But it felt as if my face was really burning, most of all on the right-hand side and at the top of my cheekbone. It was also most painful on the tip of my tongue and lips, where the sensation always started."

In November 1991 she stopped watching TV. In December she began to have equally strong symptoms from fluorescent lighting as from screens. She also reacted to direct light from light bulbs and sunlight. In January 1992 her hypersensitivity simply exploded. She went to the company doctor who put her on the sick list, saying that she had changes "similar to acne rosacea" in her skin. Acne rosacea was the usual diagnosis given when patients showed distended blood vessels, redness, and facial swelling after using VDUs. This diagnosis was sometimes given as soon as a patient mentioned the word "computer screen" and was, one might say, a "politically correct" diagnosis. No skin specialist dared to take an independent position with respect to the phenomenon. Everyone pretended there wasn't a cloud in the sky.

An occupational injury claim was lodged. On the claim form Eija Salmela wrote "general hypersensitivity to electricity that produces light, as well as to sunlight." She stayed with her mother in Finland for three months and the symptoms disappeared almost entirely. In April 1992 she returned to work at the State Power Corporation in Stockholm. She soon felt smarting pains in her face when exposed to the fluorescent lighting in corridors and to sunlight. She began to wear dark glasses. After a couple of days she was forced to stay at home. Now symptoms arose in her face and hands when exposed to lamps, electrical devices, and sunlight. Suddenly she was unable to use the phone.

Her employer arranged for her to sit in a specially sanitized room at the National Environment Protection Board – at the time there were several projects being conducted in State authorities to facilitate rehabilitation of personnel who had become sick whilst using VDUs. In May 1992 Eija Salmela wrote in her diary: "Tried going for a walk in the middle of the day but couldn't, the light was too bright, too strong… I couldn't be outdoors if it was sunny, nor indoors if the lighting was fluorescent. When close to the fridge one of my arms went numb. In the end I couldn't stand it any longer."

She had no relatives in Sweden and went back to her mother's home in Finland on 20 May that year. Here she lived in a caravan in the yard outside her parental home in the village called Räyrinki. Inside the house there was a fridge, a freezer, and a TV that she couldn't stand. After a month in the caravan she began to feel better. To her great relief the summer was rainy. In the autumn she moved into the house, after the fridge and the freezer had been moved to an outhouse. In January 1993 she noted that the symptoms had become fainter and that she only felt them when she went to the bank, post office, or shops:

I was very careful with electricity throughout the whole winter. We only used one light bulb, otherwise using candles for lighting. I began to hope that I would recover my health. But in April I made a mistake. Some trees in the garden were cut down and I went outside to watch. The sun was shining on white snowdrifts. I was about to experience the very worst period of my illness.

It all began in mid-April. First I had pains in my cheekbones

– worst on my right-hand side. The same aches and sharp pains that I had felt earlier when near to electrical devices started again and lasted for increasingly long periods. By 1 May I hardly dared to venture outside. Pains in my neck and shoulders that had always been part of my symptoms got worse – it felt as though I was carrying weights on a yoke.

Within a month Eija Salmela had developed total sensitivity to light. She moved to an attic room where the windows were covered with thick layers of dark curtains. Her mother brought up food on a tray.

> Worst of all, it felt as though even darkness was not enough to protect me, even though I stayed in the room around the clock. When the sun shone on the part of the house where the room was situated it felt as though it penetrated the walls. I was forced to try to hide behind wardrobe doors. Pain was constant in all the parts of my body that hurt when I had been exposed to VDUs. I especially remember the weighty feeling across my shoulders, as if the straps of a rucksack had dug deeper and deeper into them.
>
> It was difficult to explain this to relatives and villagers. I had become a member of the Swedish association for electrosensitive people. They sent me supplies of vitamin A and letters of encouragement. I remember crying when I received them.

Step by step, Eija Salmela succeeded in moving out of the attic room. On 29 June she was able to venture out into the pale light of Finnish summer nights for the first time. On 23 July she noted: "Free from symptoms if I don't expose myself to light." But the same month she began to have heart symptoms and her hands began to shake. She went to hospital for laboratory tests. It was found that she had far too many thrombocytes (blood platelets). The level of thrombocytes was at its highest in August, not falling to close to normal before spring 1999.

In this context it is of interest that thrombocytes contain serotonin, a substance that could form the hormone melatonin, which steers our bio-rhythm. Light and other electromagnetic radiation can affect this process. Olle Johansson explains further that this thrombocyte-derived serotonin is perhaps capable of interaction with the cutaneous serotonin-containing melanocytes.

Eija Salmela has now lived in Finland for more than ten years. During this time her symptoms have eased. Her mother has become older and ill. She is happy to have her daughter at home. Everyone in the village has known Eija since she was a little girl. No one questions her mental health – even though they think she is suffering from a remarkable illness.

> I am almost free from my symptoms now. I can stand light bulbs, can vacuum clean and use an electric whisk, we can use the electric oven, I can stand the central heating boiler, which runs on oil, as well as the circulation pump and I have never had problems with my old car.
>
> On the other hand I do have problems with fluorescent lighting, TV, and sunshine. So we don't have a TV at home. It is really fluorescent lighting that limits my life nowadays. My skin reddens and I get sharp pains as well as symptoms on the tip of my tongue when I expose myself to it. I always wear a hat in the summer and a cap with a brim if I go further afield. One worry that I still have is the high level of thrombocytes in my blood, but the level is only a little too high now and it doesn't make a great deal of difference. But I still go for regular check-ups.
>
> Earlier I used to go for long walks and bike rides but the skin on my cheeks can't stand cold and wind.

Lack of money, too, has restricted Eija Salmela's life. Many of the villagers perhaps think that she has a disability pension, she says.

> But I haven't even applied for a disability pension, as I know it's not possible to get one. Perhaps they might suggest a psychiatric

diagnosis and award me a pension based on that, but I don't even want to consider it. So far I've managed on my savings but now they're gone. What's left is six months salary due to me when I left the State Power Corporation in Stockholm. I had thought I'd use the money to buy a car if I could start to study or get another job. But it is perhaps unrealistic to think of studying – there is fluorescent lighting everywhere.

For the present the local government has promised to pay her a small salary for taking care of her mother. For two years she helped take care of another elderly person and got a small income from that. Eija Salmela leads a quiet life. She knits jumpers, dyes wool yarn using vegetable dyes, tends her kitchen garden, and takes care of her mother. Sometimes she helps to bake buns and serve coffee at church socials in the village. Most people living nearby are older than she is. "It can be a bit boring at times but most of the time I'm quite content. I'm not as young as I used to be either and my hair is turning gray. But to most of my neighbors I'm a youngster!"

This illustrates the decisive importance of a VDU in Eija Salmela's life. No matter whether it is a question of radiation in some form or chemicals emitted from it that made her ill, she has had to take the consequences; the manufacturers have not been held to their responsibility.

Her claim for occupational injury compensation was rejected.

The stories of the two women in this chapter has striking similarities with the stories about the Svenska Fläkt workers and others suffering from light sensitivity. But the women's cases were connected with computer screens. That's the difference and the reason why they couldn't be economically compensated.

6

Lamps – sources of toxic emissions

Who could have imagined that household lamps emit formaldehyde, phenol, toluene, 1-butanol, cresol, and other chemicals? But they do! And it wasn't watchdog authorities that found this out. It was one private individual who became suspicious and arranged for tests of emissions from two lamps, a common light bulb and a low-energy lamp.

This is what happened: A man called Peter had pondered for a long time over the reason that he had various signs of hypersensitivity when close to fluorescent lights, low-energy lamps, and even common light bulbs. He suffers from asthma and had noticed that the symptoms relating to his illness worsened as evenings progressed. Other people he knew, who also suffered bouts of asthma, had noticed the same thing, that their symptoms became increasingly worse in the evenings.

During the late winter/early spring of 2001, Peter had changed from bulb sockets made of plastic, which he suspected, to ceramic sockets in different lamps around his home, as he had become more and more aware of chemical emissions in general. The measures he had taken led to his being relatively free from symptoms. But one evening, whilst he was sitting reading under the light from a table lamp he started to suffer from asthma. As luck would have it there was a balcony right beside him. He decided to move the lamp outside, so that the light from it came through the balcony window. This helped. The symptoms disappeared and he could continue reading, using the light from the same lamp, coming through a windowpane.

Now he began to wonder. He had changed the socket in the lamp from a plastic to a ceramic one, and yet he had suffered his usual symptoms once again. It couldn't be the case that something in the light bulb assembly itself contained chemicals? Or could it? His guess proved to be correct.

Peter arranged for the Swedish International Testing and Research Institute in Borås to test for emissions of chemicals from lamps. Emissions from a 23W low-energy lamp and a regular 75W light bulb were measured – two common types of lamp, both made by major, well-known manufacturers. The chemists at the laboratory were surprised and skeptical. "Nothing is emitted from lamps," they said. They were even more surprised by the results, which showed that common lamps, which people use every day, actually contain and emit numerous chemicals, some of which are known to be both carcinogenic and endocrine disturbing, affecting fertility. The chemists found phenols and other substances that can cause hypersensitivity to light and many other chemicals such as formaldehyde, toluene, cresol, 1-butanol, and 4H-1.3 benzodioxin.

In autumn 2001, after the results had been made public, a battle over measuring methods and permissible values broke out in *Ny Teknik*, a Swedish technical journal. Manufacturers had stated that their lamps were not harmful to people. The only substances their lamps contained were calcium carbonate and "perhaps a little formaldehyde," as they put it.

One of the manufacturers admitted that measurements on chemicals in their lamps had been carried out in Germany. Obviously they had feared that chemicals in lamps could be a problem. The company announced that the value for formaldehyde "lay under the values permissible in work environment in Germany". But, in the case of formaldehyde, for example, it has been shown in Swedish investigations that people who have become sensitized in "sick buildings" react to infinitively much lower levels than those permissible.

Anyone who knows anything about how permissible values are set is aware that no company in the world can guarantee that its products are not harmful by referring to these values. Permissible levels are always arrived at via many compromises, often based on doubtful grounds to begin with. Furthermore, the authorities setting permissible levels always take the consequences on the national economy into consideration. When it comes to substances that disturb the endocrine system there is no firmly established dose-response link. This is something manufacturers have no wish to consider.

But how does a hypersensitive person react in an environment with 50–60 lamps, where largely similar chemicals are emitted from other electrical or electronic devices, too? We must take the duration of exposure into consideration as well as individual susceptibility. Naturally, a person who already suffers from asthma, or has other symptoms of hypersensitivity, will react more quickly. But we are all exposed to low doses of a variety of substances that enter our bloodstreams and can be stored in our fatty tissues, not to mention that they can be hormone disruptive.

Almost all the people suffering from electro- and chemical hypersensitivity I have talked with have told me that they feel sick when close to strip lighting. In all the scientific reports I have read on electro-hypersensitivity, fluorescent lighting is mentioned as one cause of trouble, but without further analysis of the factors connected with them that might provide an explanation.

With few exceptions, hypersensitive people have said that they couldn't even stand light bulbs from the beginning of their illness. But, no one has regarded lamps as being a primary cause of symptoms. They have, however, been seen as a triggering and sustaining factor once hypersensitivity has occurred.

That these chemicals are present in electrical and electronic devices, which, at the same time, create different types of electromagnetic fields and radiation, not to mention heat, are factors that have not been debated at all. Just as is the case with VDUs, as soon as one begins to find out more facts about lamps and light, one notices that it is a complex issue. It isn't only one factor that may give rise to symptoms, it can be a question of many different and interactive factors.

What if UV radiation plays a more important role than has hitherto been thought? Skin that has been affected by a combination of UV light, other electromagnetic radiation and chemicals perhaps can tolerate no radiation of any kind? Peter had been searching for a lamp that did not emit UV light. Finally he called Osram's technical department in the UK and got the answer that such a lamp does not exist. All lamps emit UV to some degree. The brighter the lamp shines, the more UV it emits.

The question of UV light from computer screens was dropped rather early. The radiation was seen as being so small that it wasn't necessary to continue checking it out. I remember the female bank clerk, the pilot case mentioned before, whose claim went through the entire legal apparatus, the result being that her skin changes and skin symptoms "not could be caused by computer screens". During the ten years that the legal proceedings continued she acquired research reports and other documentation that could have been relevant to her case, but the authorities' experts dismissed every conceivable kind of explanation and made no effort to examine possible combinations of causes.

Quite early on, she began to wonder if UV radiation from screens really was as negligible as the authorities wanted to pretend. Her skin doctor had told her that her injuries were similar to those from UV light and x-rays. She wasn't the sunbathing type and, as far as she knew, hadn't been exposed to x-rays.

x-rays are produced in VDUs, but technical experts have explained that the glass fronts of screens stop them, that no radiation that is of importance to health comes out. However, early reports from both the USA and Sweden, from tests on TV sets with the same kind of cathode ray tubes and glass fronts as computer screens, showed that the glass fronts had let through x-rays above the maximum permitted levels. This had happened accidentally when too high a voltage had occurred. Screens should normally switch themselves off after half a minute in this state.

Perhaps it seems far-fetched to speculate about possible manufacturing defects in individual VDUs, but one should bear in mind that no systematic investigations have been carried out on the screens that were used by people who suffered chronic injuries and symptoms. It has often been the case that manufacturers have quickly withdrawn screens used by people who have become sick. It is true to say that people who happened to have occupational injuries at an early stage when operating VDUs will never be recompensed. If it is the case that they happened to be using defective screens, the circumstantial evidence is already on the scrap heap. The same is true of older lamps and fluorescent lighting with, for example, PCB. If it wasn't something as serious as x-rays that had caused the skin changes in the pilot case, what about UV radiation? All the experts involved had explained to her that the UV radiation coming from her screen was not even as harmful as, for example, daylight coming through a window.

One of the professors who had provided written evidence to the court had tried to maintain that her symptoms, which were at their worst during November–December, were caused by the pale light of winter that filtered through the window of the bank where she worked. As window glass stops UV-B, he must have been thinking of UV-A.

If we believe that it is true that she did react to this pale light we immediately have to ask ourselves what caused her to be so sensitive to light. But, during the court case, no mention was made of chemicals that cause hypersensitivity to light. Another acknowledged UV expert, Professor Gunnar Swanbeck, had written to the court that low levels of UV-B-radiation could occur from screens, but that it was so faint that if one sat directly in front of a screen for eight hours one would be exposed to "equally as much UV-B as when outdoors in the middle of a summer day for ten seconds". He confirmed, however, that the woman in the pilot case did have the kind of skin injuries that usually result from exposure to UV radiation.

He didn't mention anything about UV-A radiation, which is said to be the dominant emission from screens. The risks of UV-A have been discussed in connection with halogen lamps, solariums, and PUVA-treatment for psoriasis. UV-A does penetrate through window glass. Many of those afflicted have told me that they react to light coming through windows. It is difficult to say if it is UV-A or visible light that they react to. The wavelength of visible light is in the range 400–800 nanometers.

Now the pilot case is buried in the Swedish court archives. Shortly before her case was decided in court the bank employee contacted a private expert who examined the UV measurements on VDUs made by the Radiation Protection Institute in Stockholm. He found that the Institute's experts had used such coarse methods for measuring that one could expect that they had missed that there could be UV-C radiation from the VDUs. But neither the bank employee's trade union lawyer nor the court bothered to investigate this further.

In the case of fluorescent tubes, the latest Swedish documentation of UV radiation is dated 1979. Lars-Eric Paulsson, a physicist in the section for non-ionizing radiation at the Institute of Radiation Protection in Stockholm, wrote this report. When I phoned him it became apparent that he had not dealt with the question since 1979. The authorities have trusted manufacturers to carry out control of their own products.

Yet it was the case that the 20-year-old study had been initiated when it had accidentally been found that some fluorescent tubes emitted so much UV-B radiation that exposure for a full working day at an office could cause erythemas (reddening) of the skin. UV-B has wavelengths of 280–315 nanometers; it is this type of radiation that gives us sunburn.

About 25 per cent of the 53 different types of fluorescent tubes Lars-Eric Paulsson tested were potentially capable of producing an erythema within eight hours at an illumination of 2000 lux (lux is a measurement of light strength) if used in fittings with UV-reflecting interiors and without plastic covers.

In the discussion part of his report, Lars-Eric Paulsson writes that emissions including UV-B radiation occurred, but that the amount was highly variable between different types, makes, and individual tubes. The glass in the tube was shown to be the major contributor to this variability. UV-A radiation, which has wavelengths of some 315–400 nanometers and is usually called long-wave, was emitted from all the tubes he tested. He points out that reflection from the tube fittings, ceilings, and walls may well shorten the time it takes for reddening to occur in the skin.

There are, as mentioned before, no lamps that are completely free from UV radiation emissions. Lars-Eric Paulsson writes: "Artificial sources, e.g. different devices with electrical discharges in gases, can produce substantial amounts of UV radiation of all wavelengths." He also writes that from a radiation protection standpoint it is not clear how to handle this type of exposure: "An obvious first step is to eliminate the risk of an acute erythema after one working day's exposure."

More than ten years ago there was a debate in Sweden about UV radiation from halogen lamps. The Swedish Radiation Protection Institute sent out a press release giving the information that halogen lamps emit small amounts of UV radiation if they are not given a protective glass cover. The press release stated: "... during normal use, a fitting with a bare lamp does not cause chronic injury but illumination of the skin should be avoided as it gives an unnecessary UV-dose." The Institute added that they did not recommend the use of halogen lamps as table lamps or working area lighting. Over eight hours, radiation from a 50W halogen lamp, at a distance of half a meter, is equivalent to an hour's summer sunshine. Most common halogen lamps have this effect.

At the same time, Danish measurements had also resulted in the detection of short-wave UV-C radiation from halogen lamps. An account of the measurements is given in a publication from Lyseteknisk Selskab (Lighting Technology Association) in Denmark. UV-C radiation, found at wavelengths of 200–280 nanometers, doesn't normally reach us from the sun, being absorbed before it reaches the earth's surface. But it is produced in artificial lighting. The Danish measurements were on what is called a "freely illuminating" halogen lamp. It is perhaps not so remarkable that many people have said they react strongly to halogen lamps.

If the visible light from various apparatuses contains a lot of blue light – as some fluorescent lighting and greenhouse lighting – it can injure the retina and cause skin to age more rapidly. Eye surgeons who have operated on patients using microscopes and strong blue lighting have contracted injuries to their retinas. Halogen lamps and fluorescent lighting have to have filters to hinder blue light.

In his book *Terminal Shock*, published in 1985, the Canadian Bob DeMatteo refers to Professor Emeritus William T. Ham at Virginia Commonwealth University in Richmond, USA, who found that the blue light in the visible light spectrum can cause photochemical wounds in the retina. In a 1983 issue of the *Journal of Occupational Medicine* he noted that the retina becomes more sensitive to injury when the eye is exposed to light in the blue portion of the spectrum: "Both the retina and the lens should be protected throughout life from both blue light and near UV radiation," he wrote.

If visible light is sufficiently strong it can give rise to measurable heating in the eye, Bob DeMatteo points out. He writes that a VDU operator doesn't only look directly into the light emitted from the screen but also light that is reflected by the screen. "Since the emitted light from a VDT is pulsating, it can possibly cause epileptic seizures in those predisposed to photosensitive epilepsy (seizures following stimulation by pulsating light)." This often breaks out early in life and we now know of children and young people to whom this has happened whilst sitting in front of their computer screens.

Swedish occupational safety authorities warn people who are sensitive to light-sensitizing substances not to expose themselves to UV light. The standards set may then be insufficient. But what information is there available about which substances react when subjected to UV light? No authority has warned VDU operators that they may be exposed to light-sensitizing substances from their computer equipment or other devices in office environments, even from fluorescent and other sources of light. Everyone knows that skin reddens and becomes stretched and that we get burns from too much ultraviolet light. The same symptoms have been reported by VDU operators, even something that resembles sunburn except for light areas under the nose and chin.

We know that chemicals are emitted both from VDUs and lamps. When some of them absorb energy from light they can be converted into poisonous substances and absorbed by our skin, or inhaled. Then they may very quickly enter the bloodstream.

In the worst-case scenario, when we already have poisons in our bloodstream, and we are exposed to microwaves from, for example, mobile phones, the microwaves can open our blood–brain barrier so that proteins transporting these poisons can enter our brains (see Chapter 10).

7

Flicker-rate, frequencies, fillings

Nobody seems to like flickering light. Experiments have shown, hardly unexpectedly, that electro-hypersensitive people react more strongly than control subjects. The electro-hypersensitive have an imbalance in their autonomic nervous system. There can be many reasons to this, for example chemicals and radiation. Genetic explanations are rather far-fetched when, for example, all secretaries in one workplace and 60 technicians in another become sick in front of their VDUs at the same time.

It's like jumping out of the frying pan into the fire. That was how many of the electro-hypersensitive people said they felt when fluorescent lighting with high frequency starters were installed in their offices. Older strip lighting flickered in a visible manner; with higher frequencies the flickering was less noticeable. It didn't go away but became changed to a higher frequency that the eye and brain couldn't notice as easily.

The background to these new installations was experiments that showed that electro-hypersensitive people reacted more strongly to flickering light than control groups. But even the "healthy volunteers" in the experiments found flickering unpleasant. That those already sensitized reacted most strongly was hardly unexpected. But the problem was that the electro-hypersensitive employees couldn't stand the high frequency electromagnetic fields either. And these were increased by the new lighting. Sensitivity to visible flickering could be proven, that to electromagnetic fields couldn't. This, from a purely scientific viewpoint, does not mean that such hypersensitivity doesn't exist. In a newly published book in Swedish, Clas Tegenfeldt, MSc, takes up the dilemma that various experiments in the field are simplified, above all in the media. The title of his book, *Tål du el?* means "Can you stand electricity?" Tegenfeldt writes that when researchers don't find any link between different factors it is said to prove that no connection exists, which is drawing premature conclusions. That electromagnetic fields do have biological effects is an old truth. But, writes Clas Tegenfeldt, finding the underlying mechanism(s) with respect to health is like looking for a needle in an invisible haystack that is constantly moving. Quite simply, one doesn't know what to measure, or where to look. Occasional findings are blown up out of all proportion, being given greater importance than they are really worth.

Roger Wibom, an engineer at the National Institute of Working Life in Stockholm, found that electro-hypersensitive people reacted strongly to flickering light. Even though he didn't come to any far-reaching conclusions the media presented his findings as if they explain the riddle of electro-hypersensitivity. And lamp manufacturers were delighted by the opportunity of launching a new kind of lamp onto the market.

The researchers Kjell Hanson Mild, Monica Sandström and Eugene Lyskov at the National Institute for Working Life in Umeå have noticed that electro-hypersensitive people react more to flickering than others. But they have also observed that people in this group are generally more sensitive when compared with control groups to light, sound, and vibrations. Their autonomic nervous system is in imbalance. The researchers suggest that, at least partially, this is a question of genetic factors. Kjell Hanson Mild has suggested that this category of patients ought to be treated using beta receptor blocking pharmaceuticals to dampen their hypersensitivity, which he wants to refer to as "neurophysiological circulatory disturbances". Other researchers, for example Olle Johansson at the Karolinska Institute, regard such medication as fraught with undesirable consequences; naturally, it would block the warning signals, but, in extension, also lead hypersensitive persons to expose themselves to things they can't tolerate. This could lead to further harm. In addition, Olle Johansson says that the autonomic nervous system reacts abnormally in many different circumstances, not only because of radiation and chemicals but also because of inflammations and high temperatures. The reactions are indications that something is wrong, not an explanation.

I have written about different clusters of cases of illnesses at various workplaces. There are numerous such examples to show that the hypothesis using genetic explanations is far-fetched. There must be an environmental explanation when all eight secretaries at one workplace fall ill when new computers are installed, or when 60 technicians at another place of work become almost simultaneously ill. This type of cluster has been found in many countries, even as early as when a link between miscarriages and using computers was under discussion.

There are also clusters within many families. The latest I've had contact with is a retired couple in a Swedish country town. They have become afflicted by such severe hypersensitivity to light that they don't dare to leave their home unless it's cloudy, and they are forced to keep the blinds drawn during daytime. The couple had dreamed of traveling abroad when they retired. Instead they are prisoners in their own home. The husband, a former construction engineer, told me that they suspect that one cause could be reading lights and other lighting at their former places of work and at home. They have used low energy lamps with frequency transformers for many years. Their complaints started with itching and pricking feeling in their skin, hypersensitivity to light developing later.

It just isn't possible to explain the riddle of electro-hypersensitivity by flickering or general sensitivity to various "stimuli." Something special has happened when VDUs, other electrical devices, and strip lighting have been introduced into our environments. Symptoms have broken out following this. It is here we should start looking. But why doesn't everyone become affected, is what people often ask. Not everyone suffers from allergies or gets cancer. This shouldn't stop us from looking for the causes of these illnesses.

Martin Andersson, a technician who has sanitized many workplaces at which people were having problems with VDUs and fluorescent lighting, points out that modern, high-frequency strip lighting has five times stronger alternating electric fields compared with older models.

Sanitization measures began to be taken in the 1980s with the introduction of a filter for the electrostatic fields around computer screens. It was thought that the static fields contributed to an accumulation of particles on the screens and even the VDU operators. One of the filters on the market proved itself to be superior to all others for the people who had begun to have problems with skin rashes and other complaints. This filter, produced by the American company where Martin Andersson was employed at the time, not only took away the static fields but also the alternating electric fields and electromagnetic frequencies, even those in the microwave band. The filter had previously been ordered for the armed forces but now became useful for electrohypersensitive people! The military authorities wanted to protect the high frequency bands that were used to transfer information and which, using appropriate equipment, could be picked up by an enemy.

Suspicions had arisen that alternating electric fields played at least a part in causing skin complaints suffered by VDU operators. Then research reports came from Professor Denis L. Henshaw at Bristol University, UK. He has shown that alternating electrical fields and not just static electrical fields can increase deposits of pollution particles on various electrical devices and installations. He is especially interested in concentrations of radon daughters, the decomposition products of radon, and pollutants from traffic. His opinion is that the increased occurrence of cancer in connection with electromagnetic fields, shown in numerous studies, may not only depend on the fields themselves, but also on the effect they have on chemical and radioactive particles in polluted air.

In some scientific studies a connection has been observed between skin rashes and increased levels of alternating electric fields in office environments. A Norwegian researcher, Gunnhild Oftedal, showed that if filters were earthed there was a clear reduction of skin complaints among VDU operators. But, nowadays, earthing isn't that simple, says Martin Andersson. The protective earthing of the net is seriously contaminated by signals from modern electronic equipment. As early as 1991, he and a colleague, Leif Westlund, wrote a book with the title *Hypersensitivity to electricity – can it be prevented?* It was a slim volume based on experience of concrete measures taken. The authors maintain that problems arise when high frequency electromagnetic fields are introduced into environments. One quotation from the book:

> Compared to the 50 cycles signal we have always had in most electrical appliances we now get frequencies of tens of thousands of Hz with associated harmonics. Our exposure to this is increasing dramatically with the introduction of new technology.

In the book Andersson and Westlund try to reflect, in technical terms, what has taken place in the field of electrical equipment, e.g. VDUs, lighting, photocopiers, etc. In the mid-1980s Sweden had a heated debate concerning VDUs. Demands were voiced for the reduction of electromagnetic and electrostatic emissions. "Low-emission computers" became a familiar term in voluntary testing.

Electrostatic fields were eliminated almost by 100 per cent and the magnetic fields in line frequency were substantially reduced. But, despite this, the number of people affected by hypersensitivity to electricity increased dramatically. No debate whatsoever took place about the emission of chemicals from electronic devices. The only really effective cure was for the people in question to stop working in front of VDUs. Even those in authorities such as the National Institute for Working Life admitted as much in a report published in 1989: "Stopping working with VDUs was the most well-tried, and similarly the most effective method of reducing symptoms. Changing to a low-emission computer usually did not lead to improvements – on the contrary, in several cases deterioration was noted."

Martin Andersson and his colleagues saw that it was the high frequencies from screens that gave problems. They made the same observation with respect to fluorescent tubes. Ordinary electric bulb lighting, with a frequency of 50 Hz, did not normally cause any irritation. But, when a thyristor was connected to the lighting, or when it was replaced by a high-frequency ignition fluorescent tube, problems arose. In an office environment, two of four employees started to get skin irritation after a replacement of fluorescent lighting. Measurements, made by Andersson and Westlund, revealed that the new fittings were of a high-frequency type and that they were installed with the existing cables, to which the old fluorescent lighting used to be connected, with no protective earth. This meant that the entire fitting acted as an aerial for high-frequency signals. When the fittings had been earthed the symptoms disappeared.

Perhaps it should be said that nothing in the above excludes the possibility that chemical emissions may have played a great, even decisive role. At higher frequencies, emissions of chemicals probably also increased. But, above all, this shows how complex this question is.

Also, background-illuminated LCD-screens (LCD = Liquid Crystal Display) give problems. In one case, Andersson and

Westlund could measure a high frequency signal of 68.9 kHz from such an LCD-screen, which had given skin problems to two of four employees. They also give examples that PCs with gas plasma displays gave the same type of problems before alternating electric fields were screened. When sanitizing such screens in Sweden, the strip lighting is replaced by electric light bulbs. Martin Andersson also says that it has happened that he has been called to workplaces at which he has found fluorescent lighting to be the only problem:

> Of course, fluorescent tubes also emit chemicals, but I think it is the high frequencies that cause the greatest problems. We have had 50 Hz for a hundred years, but when we started using thyristor trigger control units, in the 1960s and 1970s, we began to get high-frequency "spikes" and transients, overtones that caused problems.

In contrast to continuous fields, there are transients, or overtones, which occur when switching on and off. These transients can give rise to short-term, high-frequency fields. "One example is that a fluorescent light tube can give off a wide range of frequencies, even as high as in the megahertz area. But overtones, transients, are difficult to measure and researchers in the field have not managed to do so," says Martin Andersson.

A Swedish lighting expert, Bertil Fogelstrom, noticed that fluorescent lighting had often been a triggering factor when VDU operators began to feel ill.

> It happened that people had worked in rooms without having problems until the strip lighting was changed. It also occurred that people had worked in rooms with strip lighting without problems until a VDU was installed in the room. Then, problems started. I think it depends on the different frequencies emitted

from tubes and VDUs. Perhaps people don't feel well if they are exposed to many different frequencies at the same time.

There may be a lot of truth in his observation that a mixture of different frequencies can be important with respect to the chronic symptoms that many employees get in office environments. Symptoms often break out when changes take place, for example when a person gets a new VDU. It may depend on the higher initial emission of chemicals to begin with, but an important factor could be that the new screen has other frequencies.

Is it the case that people get used to certain frequencies and, thereafter, have difficulties in tolerating other ones? The reactions of hypersensitive people often make other people wonder and arouse mistrust. Closer examination most often shows that there are rational explanations, says Axel Ohlsson, a retired engineer who has worked at Bofors in Karlskoga, where he came into contact with many employees who had problems from VDUs:

> I know an engineer working in a hi-tech factory, where he had used PCs for many years without any problems. In connection with a survey of computer capacity in the plant he was provided with a powerful computer with a number of built-in features. After a short period he began to be troubled by a rash on his throat as well as on the hand he used to hold the mouse. The rash disappeared when he was not at work. Soon afterwards he experienced discomfort from fluorescent lighting as well as from his TV at home. Neither the rash nor other problems arose when working with his old computer.
>
> Obviously there was a decisive difference between the equipment used. So the specialist at the factory measured the occurrence of electromagnetic signals. A huge difference was observed in the emission of high frequency signals in the interval 20–1000 megahertz. It should be noted that, in general, for some reason, only signals of up to 400 kilohertz (0.4 megahertz)

coming from electronic equipment and other installations have previously been measured.

Ragnar Forshufvud, MSc, writes about electromagnetic pollution or electro-smog in his book *Bostad och hälsa*, in English "Housing and health". He calls it "this ever-present cacophony of signals, intentionally transmitted information mixed together with unintentionally spread electronic scrap". This makes me think of Bob DeMatteo, the Canadian who wrote *Terminal Shock* in 1985. Of the synergistic effects from VDUs, i.e. different effects in combination, he writes that the combined action of fields at different frequencies is more dangerous than when each field is considered independently:

> Studies show the biological damage is greater when exposures to radio frequencies and x-rays occur at the same time. The pre-treatment of tissue with microwaves enhances the effects of x-ray exposure. This is why heat packs are applied to cancer patients undergoing x-ray radiation therapy. A reinforcing of the biological effect was also found for the successive exposure to radio frequency fields and ultraviolet radiation.

It might be thought that most things have already been said in Bob DeMatteo's book. He mentions synergistic effects with chemicals as well as noise: "Noise in the workplace increases the body's vulnerability to the toxic effects of the solvent trichloroethylene."

Thereby, each exposure situation becomes unique. In winter 2001, five of Sweden's most well known researchers into the effects of electromagnetic fields, Kjell Hanson Mild, Yngve Hamnerius, Lennart Hardell, Matts-Olof Mattsson, and Monica Sandström writing in a debate article in a Swedish medical journal, *Läkartidningen*, say that exposure to magnetic fields "can be compared to exposure to several chemicals at the same time," that it is a question of a mixture of different frequencies. Their article was really about the extremely low frequency electromagnetic fields, ELFs, around power lines and electrical devices of various kinds that have now been classified as "possibly carcinogenic" by WHO, the World Health Organization. WHO's cancer research center IARC, the International Agency for Research on Cancer, decided to classify static and extremely low-frequency electric and magnetic fields as possibly carcinogenic, in autumn 2001. IARC classifies cancer risks in four levels; ELF-fields were placed in the same group, 2 B, as DDT, lead, diesel, petrol, and welding fumes. Caffeine, mercury, and fluorescent lighting are placed in the class below, group 3.

NIEHS, the National Institute of Environmental Health Sciences in the USA, has reached the same conclusions as IARC. A Californian State Committee goes even further; in an evaluation of low-frequency electric and magnetic fields they have assessed the risks for child leukemia as a few per cent greater than IARC does, also taking up other effects such as brain tumors in adults, miscarriages, and ALS (amyloid lateral sclerosis).

What then ought to be, and can be, measured concerning electromagnetic fields? It is easy to become confused by all the terms, hypotheses, theories, and opinions. One factor that isn't usually measured with respect to computer screens in Sweden is what is known as time derivatives. These time derivatives are a measure of the rate of change in field strengths per second. In the TCO-labeling of screens there are no requirements for such measurements to be taken in order to certify devices. This makes it difficult for laymen to know which screens are safest in this respect.

That time derivatives can have importance is shown in the following. In 1992, Thomas Örtendahl and Per Högstedt, two Swedish researchers, showed that certain types of screens have the effect of hastening the discharge of particles of mercury from amalgam fillings. As early as the 1980s, Thomas Örtendahl, a dental surgeon at the University Hospital in Gothenburg, had found that amalgam fillings are affected by electromagnetic fields. He had been asked to investigate why a group of divers who were working with electric tools under water had a metallic taste in their mouths and lost their amalgam fillings unusually often. He submerged fillings in liquid in a laboratory and exposed them to the same kind of electromagnetic fields as those the divers had been exposed to and noticed that the outer layer of fillings exhibited changes and were decomposed by the fields.

Later, Thomas Örtendahl and Per Högstedt found that Ericsson and Macintosh computer screens could cause release of mercury vapor from amalgam test fillings. Information as to which brands of screens were used in these experiments was not made public until four years later, when the screens in question were no longer on the market. The researchers, however, stated from the outset that the higher the time derivatives that the screens had, the greater were the amounts of mercury they caused to be released. From other researchers we know that metal vapors can enter the brain through the nose and olfactory nerves since these are connected with the olfactory lobes of the brain via nerve axons.

There is also another way in which different kinds of poisons can enter the brain. In 1997 the Swedish researchers Leif Salford, Bertil Person, and Arne Brun showed in a study repeating the 1977 pioneering work of the American electromicroscopist, Eugene Albert, that the blood–brain barrier in mice, and probably also humans, is opened by very short exposure to high frequency electromagnetic fields in the microwave range, allowing relatively large proteins that may carry poisons to pass through.

Salford, Persson, and Brun have observed similar, but weaker, effects on the blood–brain barrier caused by even lower frequencies than microwaves. No one has clarified what this means for vDU operators. This question hasn't even been raised as a point of discussion in research contexts.

When it comes to time derivatives, no one has clarified what this means for vDU-operators either. This question has only been raised by Olle Johansson and one of his co-workers at the Karolinska Institute who, in vain, attempted to commence similar studies. They were met only by resistance. At TCO, the Swedish Confederation of Professional Employees, no one cared about the results of Örtendal's and Högstedt's study. When asked why, one ombudsman said, "members have not asked to have any information about time derivatives in the TCO-labeling of screens".

It would be interesting to know how many members knew what time derivatives were and, as a result, would have been able to request measurements of them. There must be lots of members, however, with amalgam fillings, who have had concrete experience of the importance of time derivatives. One of these is Rigmor Granlund-Lind, a Swedish high school teacher, who lives just outside Stockholm. She suspects that one cause of her electro-hypersensitivity was mercury emanating from tooth fillings whilst she was working in front of a VDU. Having begun to write a doctoral dissertation, she was happy to be able to use a computer as a technical aid. The following is her own account:

> In autumn 1984 I bought my first computer, a Microbee with keyboard and computer in the same unit, without a hard disk; a cassette recorder was needed to save text. After a while my dentist told me that my amalgam fillings had corroded rapidly. The dentist got permission from the National Health Service to change the fillings to gold. This meant that for a period I had both gold and corroded amalgam fillings in my mouth. My tongue became ulcerated and I constantly had a sore throat.
>
> Replacing the amalgam with gold made me very ill. I was put on sick leave and became weaker by the week. I was probably already electro-hypersensitive without realizing it – I had never heard of electro-hypersensitivity. Doctors diagnosed the breathing difficulties and dizziness that I was suffering from as anxiety and I was referred to a psychiatrist. I believed that the problems were psychosomatic. But the symptoms continued to get worse.

Among the symptoms I had were breathing difficulties: attacks of apnea when I had sat in front of a computer for a while. I had to force myself to breathe for several minutes. This also happened often when I tried to sleep after working in front of the computer during the day. I also had fainting sensations, dizziness, and muscle weakness. My body went into overdrive; I had a rapid pulse and an agitated mental state as well as feeling flushed in my face and having a stinging sensation in my eyes.

After a while I couldn't stand anything electrical, nor could I be outside in the sunshine – I became faint and dizzy and my face and eyelids swelled up.

It wasn't until a good friend of mine, a civil engineer and lecturer at the University Technical College in Luleå, found out about my symptoms and realized I had become electro-hypersensitive that I got the opportunity to recover my health. My friend had a colleague called Björn Hagvall, a computer supervisor at the university college who was one of the earliest known cases of electro-hypersensitivity in Sweden.

In summer 1988 Rigmor Granlund-Lind went to a dentist in Norway to have her fillings replaced. He used methods that protected her from further exposure to mercury. Within a few months she was much better.

In winter 1991, the local government in the area in which she lived, gave her financial aid to electro-sanitize her house. Up to then she had lived in darkness for almost two years with most of the fuses in her home disconnected. She had been on a research sabbatical for this period and was able to study at home in a healthy environment. But, in 1991, she went back to teaching at Nacka High School, which had carried out extensive electro-sanitization for her sake. All fluorescent lighting in one classroom had been replaced by conventional light bulbs. The slide overhead projector and tape recorder cables had been insulated using protective covering and the fluorescent lights in one corridor were screened.

Everything went well, Rigmor Granlund-Lind could carry on working; over the years she became much less electrosensitive. But, as far as possible, she tried to avoid computers, using every possible means. Her dissertation in the field of literature, which she defended in 1995, was written on an old portable typewriter. In autumn 1997 she felt well enough to buy another computer – a Macintosh that had been electrically sanitized at her request. At the same time she changed schools to work in an ordinary non-sanitized environment.

> Unfortunately, as each month passed I became more electrosensitive again. Here I was working in a classroom with fluorescent lights, non-sanitized electrical cables, and, worst of all, had to move about in school corridors where students constantly used mobile phones. I also began to react with increasingly worse symptoms in front of my electro-sanitized computer. All my earlier symptoms returned and I experienced new ones. In autumn 1999 I suffered cramp at nights and on one occasion had to be rushed to hospital by ambulance. The attacks of cramp stopped when I stopped using my electro-sanitized computer. From November 1999 I spent most of my time in my electro-sanitized house and in a vacation home with the electricity switched off. I began to recover again.

Rigmor Granlund-Lind has analyzed her symptoms critically and cannot come to any other conclusion than that she does, indeed, react to electromagnetic fields. Symptoms took her unawares on many occasions; later she became conscious of what could have caused them – sources of electromagnetic radiation being subsequently found in the vicinities where the symptoms had occurred.

8

VDUs emit triphenyl phosphate

Swedish researchers have shown that VDUs emit chemicals called triphenyl phosphates. This could explain many of the health complaints people have been experiencing. But other experts have ignored these results. This type of chemical can cause damage to red and white blood cells. The long-term effects on the population being continuously exposed to these substances in their homes and at their workplaces remain to be seen.

It was purely by accident that in 1997 possibly the most important discovery with respect to chemical emissions from VDUs was made. Chemists working at the National Institute for Working Life in Stockholm discovered that organic phosphate compounds are emitted from the plastic casings of VDUs. The compounds showed themselves as peaks of interference in laboratory tests on outdoor air samples. "At first we didn't understand where they came from, but in the end we realized that they were in the air in the laboratory," says Associate Professor Conny Östman. "We asked the National Chemicals Inspectorate what such compounds are used for, and learned that, amongst other things, they are used as flame-retardants in electronic devices. We became interested, leading to studies of office environments. This was how we found that triphenyl phosphate, used as a flame-retardant, was emitted from VDUs."

First, measurements were made in office environments with no computers, then with computers that were not switched on, and finally with computers switched on. It became obvious that triphenyl phosphate, known to have allergenic and other negative properties, was emitted solely from the computer equipment. This breakthrough happened in 1997. For the first time Swedish researchers showed that VDUs emitted something harmful that could explain the health complaints people were experiencing. But colleagues at the Institute for Working Life who were conducting research on the electromagnetic fields from VDUs did not congratulate Conny Östman and his team. They simply ignored it. "Nobody from the Institute contacted us. Lots of people must have known about our findings as they were reported as news both on TV and in newspapers. Some people who suffered from VDU-sickness phoned us, urging us to continue our research."

For several years, Professor Bengt Knave at the Institute for Working Life has been responsible for research into possible health risks from VDUs. He also organized the first international conference about VDUs in 1986. Like most other experts, he has always described VDU-sickness as a multi-factorial problem in which chemicals play a part. But collaboration with chemists has not been of interest to him, nor to others at the Institute working with this problem.

"We would have been interested in cooperating with them, but were led to believe that the chemical aspects were not seen as being important in this context," is Conny Östman's comment. Following cutbacks and some turbulence at the Institute, Conny Östman and his fellow researchers are now at the Department of Analytical Chemistry at the University of Stockholm, where they have formed a special unit for work environment chemistry. At last, after several years' delay, they have been able to conduct studies on chemical emissions from VDUs, partly within the framework of a project financed by SIF, the Swedish Union of Clerical and Technical Employees in Industry.

Now we can look more generally at compounds that are emitted from vdus, giving us a foundation to build on. We are taking special interest in screen types that have been used at workplaces at which people have experienced problems.

Fortunately, such screens had been collected from some offices by Martin Andersson, a technician whose suspicion that chemical emissions from computers play a part in this context arose in the early stages. He has sanitized many workplaces where employees have had problems and achieved noticeable improvements by encasing vdus so that electromagnetic fields are reduced and chemical emissions eliminated.

The researchers at the Department of Analytical Chemistry keep screens switched on, and collect samples of emissions from their tops, where they are hottest and most chemicals are emitted. Using different analytical methods they are attempting to find out which compounds occur. When it is established that exposure to different substances does occur, collaboration with toxicologists is important, to find out the health risks that are associated with each substance. Such collaboration has already been established, for example, with a Finnish researcher, Paavo Honkakoski at the Pharmaceutical Department at Kuopio University. In cell culture studies he has found organophosphates in nuclear receptors. The source of the chemical substances has not been identified. Conny Östman:

> We certainly don't know how people who are exposed to low concentrations of substances over longer periods of time may be affected in the long run. This is a question that, to a great extent, concerns office environments, which, up to now, have been considered free from health risks due to chemicals.
>
> We question this view, one reason being that there have been reports for many years about people experiencing trouble. We also know that it may be up to 120 degrees C inside the equipment and that emissions, at least of triphenyl phosphate, do occur.

When the researchers examined 18 screens from a single manufacturer, they found that the plastic casings contained up to 10 per cent triphenyl phosphate. For chemists who are used to running trace analyses and trying to find microscopic amounts it isn't at all usual to be in a situation where tenths of a certain substance are found. When such a screen is switched on in a small office and measurements are taken at the distance from the screen at which an operator normally sits, concentrations of triphenyl phosphate of almost 100 nanograms per cubic meter were found to be present in the air. These measurements were carried out when a newly manufactured VDU was used for the first time. After 183 days of constant use, equivalent to about two years of normal operation, the level had fallen to about 10 nanograms per cubic meter. It may be mentioned that it is possible to measure considerably higher concentrations. After using a brand-new TV for one day, concentrations of up to 250 nanograms per cubic meter of triphenyl phosphate were found in air of the room. As measurements had been made in a room without VDUs, then with VDUs that had not been switched on, and finally with devices switched on, it was established that the triphenyl phosphate found had only come from the VDUs. Ten of the 18 computer screens examined had triphenyle phosphat in the casing, even though the manufacturer had declared otherwise.

When publishing their findings, the researchers pointed out that the results may give a possible explanation for skin complaints. Triphenyl phosphate is known to be a cause of contact allergies. Some of the organophosphates that researchers at the department have studied, including triphenyl phosphate, have a hemolytic effect, meaning that they cause red blood cells to decompose. Triphenyl phosphate can, however, also affect monocytes, a kind of white blood cell that is known as a "cleansing" cell and is important in our immune defense. Workers who have been exposed to a mixture of triphenyl phosphate and isopropyl triphenyl phosphate have been found to have a lower count of this specific type of blood cells. What the long-term effects of a large proportion of the population in the industrialized world being continuously exposed to triphenyl phosphate at their workplaces and in their homes may be, remains to be seen.

Triphenyl phosphate is one of a group of organophosphate-esters that has begun to receive considerable attention recently. When plans have been made to discontinue the use of brominated flame-retardants, these organophosphate-esters have often been thought of as replacements. In fact they are extremely interesting to manufacturers as they can be used both as flame-retardants and as plasticizers. These substances, called additives, meaning that they are not bound up by plastic, are used not only in electronic devices but also in a number of contexts, including building materials. However, the Department for Analytical Chemistry at Stockholm University has produced several reports on organophosphate-esters that have caused numerous people to wonder if we aren't jumping out of the frying pan into the fire. In the thesis for his doctorate, Håkan Carlsson, at the Department, has proved that these organophosphate-esters occur generally as indoor air pollutants. He has studied their occurrence in an office, a children's day-care center, and in three school buildings. One of the pollutants Håkan Carlsson found was trichloro-ethylphosphate. Results given in another report show concentrations of trichloro-ethylphosphate of up to 1200 nanograms per cubic meter. This measurement was made at a children's hospital in Stockholm, where soundproofing sheets of the type used in many public buildings were identified as the source.

Trichloro-ethylphosphate is known to be neurotoxic; it affects nervous tissues. There are reports that this chemical causes brain damage to rats, a damage of a type that has not been observed earlier in connection with chemicals. This damage has occurred in parts of the brain that are important for memory. Several of the organophosphate-esters react with the enzyme acetylcholinesterase, which regulates nerve impulses to muscles, as well as to the brain in connection with memorizing and learning. If acetylcholinesterase is inhibited the autonomic nervous system is affected. In the group of chemicals known as organophosphate compounds, there are different nerve gases, amongst them the notorious sarin gas. Studies, carried out in military contexts, have shown that extremely low concentrations of these substances have an adverse effect on combat pilots' ability to react. Animal experiments show that some chlorophosphates, chlorinated organophosphate-esters, can cause lowered sperm production and ovulation. In animal studies, many of the organophosphate-esters have shown themselves to have carcinogenic effects. Hitherto, methods have not been available to measure these substances in human blood and urine and it is still unknown how they are taken up by the human body. However, the Department of Analytical Chemistry is busily attempting to produce suitable methods. It is already possible to investigate the amounts of these substances in blood samples.

Like all researchers, Conny Östman is cautious. But he doesn't deny that it is the new ailments in office environments that are among the driving forces behind his work. He feels that it is important to be able to show that the chemicals currently being debated leak out into our indoor environment. We know what effects these have had in animal studies. Now there is a basis for further study. The phosphate-esters in question are not manufactured in Sweden, but are imported in finished goods. Major chemical industries like Bayer, Akzo Nobel, Sandoz, and Monsanto produce 60,000 to 80,000 tons of these esters each year.

Many people have been led to believe that risks connected with chemicals no longer exist in working life because the risks of injuries connected with chemicals in heavy industry have been successfully dealt with. But, nowadays we have other chemicals, which, in low concentrations are found in completely different environments than those traditionally regarded as being subjected to chemical risks. Regrettably, there are far too few chemists who are working in this field of research, and governmental research grants are parsimonious.

It doesn't seem to be completely clear to the trade unions that there is no major difference in white- and blue-collar workplaces when it comes to risks linked to chemicals. Nowadays, more and more employees sit in front of the same kind of electronic equipment. Engineers and technicians handle printed circuit cards and other electronic components. Most of them work in clean environments where it might be thought that health risks have been eliminated. That this is not the case is known from what the microelectronics industry calls "clean rooms."

The Swedish Metalworkers' Union is running a project concerned with a group of chemicals called isocyanates, substances that are a starting point in the manufacture of polyurethane. The white-collar workers' unions have not yet really understood that they ought to be equally involved in this matter.

Professor Gunnar Skarping and his colleagues at the University Hospital in Lund have produced new measuring methods, capable of showing the presence of isocyanates in contexts that methods used earlier had been unable to detect. Isocyanates are found in foam plastics, rubber materials, varnishes, adhesives, insulation and sealing materials, used for example in refrigerators, cars, district heating pipes and building blocks. Heated mineral wool and Bakelite release isocyanates. In addition isocyanates are present in electronic products, above all in printed circuit cards and cables. Isocyanates are set free once the products they are used in are heated, for example during polishing, welding, or soldering. They can occur as a gas, or in the form of particles that attach themselves to dust and surfaces. "These condensation particles are especially troublesome as they can reach far down into the lungs," Gunnar Skarping says.

> In literature concerning isocyanates it is first and foremost workers in chemical industries that have been studied. The chemicals used there, how they are handled, and how they are mixed, are known. But it seems to be the case that it is entirely

different groups of people who are most exposed, people who haven't known about the problems that plastics in their environment may cause. One example is the electronics industry. Employers, too, have not been aware of the risks.

If isocyanates are inhaled, they can cause serious respiratory problems of a type referred to as isocyanate asthma. Skin can become sensitized, and headaches and rhinocleisis (blocked nasal passages) are common. But it was thought that such problems had been dealt with by not exceeding limit values set by the National Board of Occupational Safety and Health. Unions, however, noticed that problems continued to occur at places of work. Many employees became ill and it was shown that they had concentrations of isocyanates in their blood and urine – despite measurements, using methods recommended by the National Board of Occupational Safety and Health, not showing any concentrations of isocyanates at the workplaces in question.

Using the new methods of measuring produced by the research group in Lund, unions were able to tackle matters. This was the starting point for a lengthy struggle between unions and occupational safety and health authorities. In the end the Metalworkers' Union took the matter directly to the Government, demanding that action be taken. Now enormous amounts of research are required to establish the extent to which isocyanates occur and what health risks are entailed. "We import over a hundred different isocyanates to Sweden and we lack knowledge about most of them," says Gunnar Skarping.

> Even more are formed when you heat plastics. The decomposition products formed are new substances. Finding out what their various toxic qualities are would be such an extensive task that you could say it is an impossible one.

✖

The real champion of the campaign against isocyanates that

the Metalworkers' Union has conducted is Rolf Ählberg. He has retired, but continues to work on the question of isocyanates both at Nordic and European levels. As a working environment ombudsman he raised alarms on such environmental hazards as asbestos and solvents. Now he is devoting himself to the question of isocyanates. As a trade union representative he has experienced the need for unusual amounts of energy to tackle working life environment risks. Opposition is strong, not least among doctors.

> The first alarm was raised in 1977. This concerned six cases in one industry. One of them was a twenty-two-year-old woman who had been working with polyurethane foam. She had to take early retirement pension. When, via the media, the first cases became known, it was found that there were similar problems in many places; 18 employees at one factory had contracted asthma, 50 in another...
>
> At that time the old methods of measuring were still being used, but it was possible to prove that people became ill. Even if the set limits were not exceeded, at that time of course, we had a good form of occupational injuries insurance that didn't pass the burden of proof to the person affected.
>
> The National Board of Occupational Safety and Health produced new rules during the eighties and we thought we had got matters under control. But new cases kept popping up all the time. When Gunnar Skarping showed that the measuring methods had been insufficient, in 1996, we found an explanation as to why people had become ill despite our not being able to measure any concentrations of isocyanates in their workplace environments.

Recently Rolf Ählberg has primarily taken an interest in the electronics industry where people have not yet understood the risks that employees are being exposed to. This is the case for both white- and blue-collar workers, he says.

Those who solder printed circuit cards are exposed to high concentrations of isocyanates, irrespective of whether the cards are
lacquered or not. But, in most firms in the electronics industry,
people work without taking protective measures. It is frighten-
ing to see how companies ignore the findings of recent research,
despite the fact that we have produced illustrated information
to show how one can take precautions, specifically for the electronics industry.

Rolf Ählberg's words evoke associations. A remarkable number
of those hypersensitive to electricity have technical occupations.
Engineers have been over-represented from time to time in the
board set up by the association the electro-hypersensitive started.
One theory, put forward by some professors, is that this is
because they are so ambitious and stressed out. Perhaps it would
be more interesting to collate facts about what these technicians
have worked with, to find out how much soldering and cutting
they have done on printed circuit cards, without using protective
gloves and forced ventilation.

  In a brochure on isocyanate hazards in the electronics industry,
work such as lacquering, hardening, and heat treatment, soldering,
renovating, and repairing, cutting and truncating printed circuit
cards, as well as cutting and joining optical fiber and copper
cables, are all mentioned. Optical fiber cables have an acrylate
lacquer coating that contains small amounts of polyurethane; the
same is true for copper wires. "If you've become hypersensitive to
isocyanates you become intolerant to everything," Rolf Ählberg
says.

At one factory, over 40 female employees became ill. The
majority of them are so hypersensitive that, if they drive into the
parking lot outside the factory, they get respiratory problems if
the wind is blowing in their direction.

I have met one of these women. She had worked with a heat press for plastic materials, as well as a hot-air blower used for heating adhesives. She has symptoms that include pressure in her chest, severe eye and facial pains, and sensations of fainting. She has also developed hypersensitivity to different substances such as perfumes. And she is hypersensitive to light; this constantly recurring symptom among those I write about in this book: "It's strange, I can't stand sunshine when it comes through car windows, but out at sea I can stand it." This, too, I've heard before, but in connection with people who became ill whilst using VDUs.

9

New chemicals –
new illnesses

We all have brominated flame-retardants in our blood and fat tissues today. These substances can also be found in human breast milk. It is a new phenomenon, which has occurred in the last few decades. "That they are permitted makes me feel as though I've lived in vain," says a well-known Professor of Chemistry, Sören Jensen, who discovered the spreading of PCB compounds in life cycles in 1966. Professor Lennart Hardell is another researcher who fears that the increased frequency of asthma, allergies, and similar sicknesses can partly be caused by new chemicals.

Rachel Carson's book *Silent Spring* – the great classic of the 1960s – was the book that awakened the whole world to the dangers of new, synthetic chemicals. Mankind doesn't seem to have learnt much from Rachel Carson's warnings. It was, above all, DDT that she raised the alarm about. Then came the 1970s with the spreading of polychlorinated biphenyls, PCBs as they became known as. PCBs, which are as stable in the environment as DDT, consist of over 200 different chemical compounds. During recent decades the brominated flame-retardants, which are very similar to PCBs, have been given free range, without intervention by authorities. "It's outrageous that this has been allowed to happen, that nothing has been learnt from the PCB catastrophe," says Professor Emeritus Sören Jensen, Danish born, but working at Stockholm University for many years.

Sweden banned PCB in 1971. At that time we didn't even know if it was poisonous. The only thing we knew was that it was extremely stable in food chains. Those in authority held that we ought not to have such substances. Later it was confirmed that there were good reasons for such a ban. That brominated flame-retardants, which are almost as stable as PCBs, are permitted makes me feel as though I've lived in vain.

When Sören Jensen says this, we have reason to pay attention. It was he who discovered the spreading of PCB compounds in life cycles. It all began with a dead sea eagle in Stockholm's Archipelago, in 1966. Sören Jensen revealed that the bird's body contained both DDT and PCB. His sensational discovery became a global warning signal. Similar reports began to come in from many other countries.

PCB had been produced since 1929. Spreading throughout food chains had been going on for 37 years when Sören Jensen raised the alarm. PCB has been used, above all, in electrical devices, oils, in transformers and condensers, as adhesives, solvents, and softeners in PVC plastics etc. Like DDT it is soluble in fats and can be stored in the body. Liver injuries have been reported in workers who have come into contact with these substances, which are hard to break down. PCB can also affect thyroxin, a hormone produced in the thyroid gland and, thus, disturb vital parts of the human hormone system.

In the 1960s a major catastrophe occurred in Japan, where thousands of people had eaten foods contaminated with PCB; they had chronic injuries to their central nerve systems as well as skin and mucous membrane changes.

The PCB levels in the Baltic Sea were high for a long time but had begun to drop for the first time in the 1990s, when it was found that they began to increase once again. It was suspected that the Daugava, a Latvian river, carried waste from an old factory in Riga that manufactured electrical goods.

Nowadays brominated flame-retardants, closely resembling

PCB, are being spread in the food chains. We already have these substances in our blood and fatty tissues. Some time ago, Gunilla Lindström, Professor of Environmental Chemistry at Örebro University, had an interesting opportunity to compare the amounts of these poisons in the blood of present-day people with those in blood from the 1940s. Preserved blood plasma, from the 1940s, had been left lying in the cellar store of a Swedish hospital. It had originated in the USA, and was to have been used in the final stages of the Second World War, if it hadn't been contaminated with hepatitis. There were traces of PCB in this blood from the 1940s, but it was otherwise almost free from synthetic environmental toxins.

Åke Bergman, Professor at the Department of Environmental Chemistry at Stockholm University, discovered as early as 1996 that one type of brominated flame-retardant, PBDEs, polybrominated diphenyl ethers, was present in human blood. That these were widespread in nature had been known since the beginning of the 1980s, when they were found in fish. Just like PCB, PBDE is accumulated in fatty tissues and can disturb hormonal balance by blocking thyroxin. Back in 1996 Åke Bergman said that it was high time to investigate the extent to which computer users in offices were exposed to these substances. Those who worked in front of screens for lengthy periods might be at risk, at least if the devices were new, he argued.

At a conference about brominated flame-retardants held in Stockholm in autumn 2001, neonatal exposure to the polybrominated diphenyl ethers PBDE 99 and PBDE 153 was discussed. Swedish researchers have found that exposure to these substances can affect the learning and memory functions and lead to an increased susceptibility to toxic agents in adult rats. Sören Jensen again:

> When newly born mice are exposed to brominated flame-retardants at the most sensitive stage of brain development, they have carried the dose with them throughout their lives and it has made them more over-active than other mice from litters

that have not been exposed to these substances. I think this is extremely alarming.

The brain, of course, develops in different ways during different stages. In mice and rats the most vulnerable period is neonatal, spanning the first 3–4 weeks of life. The most sensitive period for human development starts prior to birth, it begins during the third trimester of pregnancy and continues throughout the first two years of life.

What could this mean for pregnant women in front of VDUs in offices?

If they are exposed to these substances their children could suffer later in life. We have noticed this with nicotine. Children who have been exposed to nicotine during the fetal period can become over-active their whole lives, that's one of the reasons why pregnant mothers shouldn't smoke.

Other researchers have irradiated brominated flame-retardants of the PBDE type, using UV light, and observed that brominated dibenzofurans and dibenzodioxins are formed. UV light also causes these substances to split off bromine. What do these phototoxic reactions mean?

We can only speculate about this, for the moment. The UV light has to be quite short waved. Sunlight at our latitude gives very slow effects. I have tried to identify what is formed when PCB is UV-irradiated. But whether or not that which is formed is more toxic than PCB is something others will have to test. We chemists, of course, need to collaborate with biologists and toxicologists.

Nowadays we have a number of symptoms of hypersensitivity, MCS (multiple chemical sensitivity) for example. Can people already have been harmed by these substances? "I can only hope it hasn't gone that far," Sören Jensen replies.

In *Silent Spring* Rachel Carson wrote that many people reckon only with chronic poisoning resulting from single, major exposures. The really big problem can, however, be the gradual storing of small quantities of fat-soluble chemicals in our bodies.

In the 1960s it was, above all, the storing of insecticides that we were warned about – not only in fatty tissues but also in individual cells. Rachel Carson stressed that this can disturb such basic functions as absorption of oxygen and generation of energy. She also warned us of the effects that poisons have on our livers, a vital organ with respect to metabolism and detoxification. If the liver becomes damaged, the body's protection against poisons is weakened. Rachel Carson pointed out that the two most important types of insecticides, chlorinated hydrocarbons and organic phosphates, have direct effects on the nervous system. DDT affects the central nervous system in human beings, which may lead to symptoms such as stinging and burning sensations in the skin, itching, trembling, and severe twitching. Researchers who tried the effects of this poison on themselves in the 1960s reported fatigue and pains in their joints. Rachel Carson comments ironically that some experts characterized the symptoms reported by the researchers as psychoneurotic. This seems remarkably similar to current comments on electro-hypersensitivity and other illnesses.

When it comes to DDT there were sufficient case descriptions in which one could see that those afflicted recovered when they were no longer in contact with the compounds, the symptoms recurring rapidly as soon as they were exposed to them again. This, in Rachel Carson's opinion, was a sufficiently serious warning, of a kind that is usually taken seriously in connection with other illnesses. Fifty years later, thousands of chemically sensitive and electro-hypersensitive people report exactly the same – that the most effective way of not having symptoms is to avoid exposing oneself to what one becomes ill from. But the official experts have only regarded this as "non-verified," anecdotal, evidence.

It is a distressing experience to read Rachel Carson's book today. Her writing includes accounts that, as early as the 1960s, some doctors noted that up to a third of their patients were suffering from some form of hypersensitivity and that the number continued to grow. That people are exposed to combinations of different poisons entails grave risks, she warned:

> Whether released into soil or water, or a man's blood, these unrelated chemicals do not remain segregated; there are mysterious and unseen changes by which one alters the power of another for harm.

Rachel Carson warned of a flood of chemicals that could give rise to new sicknesses of hitherto unknown kinds. Perhaps we have already reached this situation? I put this question to Lennart Hardell, Professor of oncology at the University of Örebro. "Yes, I think so," was his quick reply.

> Our control over new sicknesses is poor. I'm thinking of the greatly increased frequency of asthma, allergies, non-characteristic skin complaints, stress symptoms, diabetes, and other similar complaints. We have not really taken notice how things are and what links there may be with various environmental factors.

Lennart Hardell points out the remarkable lack of interest in workplace investigations from unions and authorities. Starting with the substances that are present at a workplace it should be an obvious step to measure the amounts of these in employees' blood. One problem in this context, however, is that nowadays we all have amounts of different substances such as PCB in our blood. Amounts that are regarded as being "normal" – a dangerous thought-shift as Lennart Hardell points out.

> Unfortunately, researchers and experts often lo[illegible] chemical at a time; there are practically no studies in wh[illegible] the whole mixture that we are exposed to nowadays has been gathered together – a pinch of PCB, a little dioxin, a few phthalates, etc. No one knows what the current bombardment of chemicals, taken as a whole, means for mankind. Society has extremely poor control over which chemicals are present in various products.

Multiple chemical sensitivity, MCS, hasn't been talked about in Sweden until recent years, but Lennart Hardell had one case as early as the beginning of the 1980s. This was a woman who was extremely sensitive to weed-killers. She only had to drive past a newly sprayed area to get symptoms. A debate was already going on in the USA about people who had become hypersensitive to chemical means of pest control, but the debate hadn't reached Sweden. The woman in question received no understanding whatsoever from her doctors. They regarded her complaint as being psychosomatic.

Lennart Hardell had already begun to take an interest in the carcinogenic properties of chemicals in the 1970s, when he found a connection between Hormoslyr, a commercial herbicide, and cancer of the lymph glands, non-Hodgkin's lymphoma. Hormoslyr is the same as Agent Orange, which Americans spread in Vietnam as a defoliant. Its negative effect on the Vietnamese population is known. Hormoslyr was used in Sweden from the beginning of the 1950s and into the 1970s. Some of the workers who sprayed this herbicide on unwanted vegetation got basal cell cancer on exposed areas of skin. A case study that Lennart Hardell published in 1977, showed that men who had been working with Hormoslyr had contracted an unusual form of connective-tissue tumor, sarcoma. Two years later, in a larger study, he and his co-workers found a clear relationship between sarcomas and pesticides, which resulted in one Swedish zoophysiologist accusing him of being a "prophet of doom." But in 1997, 20 years later, the World Health Organization, WHO, determined that there is a clear link between cancer and the dioxins.

Lennart Hardell recalls unpublished cases he met in connection with working with the Hormoslyr question. He remembers a 15-year-old schoolgirl who had taken a summer job, spraying Hormoslyr and had been afflicted by basal cell cancer on her back. The cancer recurred when she was in her thirties. Others had strange skin changes, redness, and skin that became thinner. These different symptoms and changes have never been reported in scientific journals, but Lennart Hardell still has the case study notes and says he intends to look through them again.

> It seemed as though the various manifestations had something to do with a combination of sunlight and Hormoslyr. They were found on parts of the skin that had been exposed to light.

Lennart Hardell and his colleagues have tried to determine which mechanisms could initiate lymph gland cancer and have, therefore, taken an interest in dioxins and chemicals such as DDT, PCB, and brominated flame-retardants. Several of these substances affect human immune defense systems and, in their studies, they have been able to observe that a combination of chemicals and viruses increases the risk of lymph gland cancer, one of the types of cancer that is currently increasing most in the Western World.

Lennart Hardell and his colleagues have studied environmental toxins in breast cancer tumors that had been removed. They have analyzed the occurrence of substances including organic compounds of chlorine, dioxins, dibenzofurans, DDT, PCB, and hexachlorobenzene. They are relatively alone in the world in studying the connections between environmental poisons and several types of cancer. With respect to lymph gland cancer, there is an American study of the connection between viruses and PCB. Otherwise, to his knowledge, nothing has been published. The research in Örebro is threatened by lack of funding. There are no funds available to go further with the analysis of substances such as phenols and phthalates, which Lennart Hardell would like to take a closer look at.

Since 1992, despite annual applications, his research has received no funding from the Swedish Cancer Society, a trust supported by many large organizations. On the other hand the privately funded Cancer Fund at the University Hospital in Örebro and the Cancer and Allergy Fund in Sweden have contributed to his project concerning chemicals and to research he has been conducting in collaboration with Professor Kjell Hanson Mild into mobile telephony and cancer. The Cancer and Allergy Fund, which, in recent years, has often been attacked for supporting controversial research, provides funding for a large part of the current Swedish environmental research. The Swedish Cancer Society, which annually allocates US $39 million to research, doesn't seem to find environmental research interesting. As far as Lennart Hardell is aware, there are no major international efforts in connection with environmental toxins and cancer, especially on combination effects from low-dose exposure to toxic chemicals in the environment.

Lennart Hardell hasn't hesitated to take part in debate when he has thought he had important facts to put forward about the risks of environmental toxins. An article, on breastfeeding and the risk for cancer in children, published in Sweden's leading daily paper in April 2001, aroused great attention. One of the co-writers was Professor Gunilla Lindström. She has shown that after six-months breastfeeding the amounts of environmental poisons such as PCB have been halved in the mother. The chemicals have been transferred to the infant, who has equally as large amounts as the mother. As the child grows, the poisons are diluted out in its fatty tissues. For the mother, breastfeeding is advantageous. Studies show that it reduces the risk of both uterine cancer and breast cancer. Instead, the risks from environmental poisons have been transferred to the infant, the authors wrote.

In the *European Journal of Clinical Nutrition*, Lennart Hardell and Gunilla Lindström have also given an account of a study of how long children afflicted by cancer had been breastfed. The period of breastfeeding has been seen as a measure of exposure to environmental toxins. With respect to all forms of cancer, taken together, no increased or decreased risk was seen for the children that had been breastfed. On the other hand they saw a fivefold increased risk for lymph gland cancer of the non-Hodgkin's lymphoma type in children who had been breastfed for 1–6 months. Children who had been breastfed for six months or longer had a sevenfold increased risk of being afflicted. Increased risk for this type of lymph gland cancer has also been found in adults, linked to substances such as brominated flame-retardants, hexachlorobenzene, and dioxins, poisons which are present in mothers' milk. In Sweden, an account of finding the brominated flame-retardant PBDE in the fatty tissues of patients with non-Hodgkin's lymphoma was given as early as 1997. The amounts of DDT and PCB in mothers' milk were at their highest during the 1960s and 1970s, whilst the amounts of brominated flame-retardants of the PBDE type are increasing all the time. Since the 1970s they have doubled every five years.

Researchers at both the National Swedish Food Administration and the Karolinska Institute have measured the amounts of brominated flame-retardants in breast milk. They found individual large differences that couldn't be explained by food intake, age, body weight, alcohol consumption, or smoking. A few women in a group of 93 who had given birth to their first baby had up to ten times the average levels. The researchers suggested electronic products as being a possible source of exposure.

That there is a connection between mobile telephony and chemicals is shown by the fact that microwaves from cell phones can open the blood–brain barrier of rats. Chemicals can thereby penetrate into the brain when this protective barrier is opened (see Chapter 10).

Even if it is primarily neurological injuries that are feared in that context, cancer is also part of the ominous scenario. In two studies Professors Lennart Hardell and Kjell Hanson Mild have shown heightened risk of brain tumors whilst using analogue NMT telephones. These mobile phones are now obsolete. In a study published in *The European Journal of Cancer Prevention* in 2002 they reported a 127 per cent higher risk for benign brain tumors in people who had used these mobile phones up to a year prior to diagnosis. After five years' use the risk had increased to 136 per cent, and after ten years 177 per cent. In all of the studies it has been found that the risk of brain tumors is greater on the side of the head that is normally used in mobile telephoning. The researchers have also noted an increased risk for malignant brain tumors. Lennart Hardell is one of the increasing number of researchers around the world who call for a limitation of the use of cell phones, above all for children and young people.

In autumn 2001, Lennart Hardell was to find out that it is just as controversial and dangerous to conduct research into the connection between cancer and electromagnetic radiation as it is to do so into cancer and environmental toxins. Five professors leveled heavy criticism against him and Associate Professor Olle Johansson at Karolinska Institute in a debate article in one of Sweden's major daily papers. They maintained that there are no causes for concern arising from any of the substances Lennart Hardell had warned about. PCB, phenoxyacetic acids, and dioxins in Hormoslyr (Agent Orange) probably constitute no risk factor whatsoever towards cancer, and the thought that cell phones might be able to cause brain tumors is "biologically bizarre." The tumors that Lennart Hardell had found in users of mobile telephones constituted "with greatest probability, a random find".

The latter was especially sensational, as one of the five professors was Anders Ahlbom, who is currently leading the Swedish part of a major international investigation of mobile telephones and the risks of brain tumors, under the auspices of the International Agency for Research on Cancer, IARC, WHO's cancer research center. Lennart Hardell reflects that perhaps Ahlbom's objectivity should be questioned if he views suspicion of possible risks involving mobile phones to be bizarre. He also comments that the same people have made this type of attack and attempted to cast suspicion on him earlier.

In September 2001, another of the five co-authors, Hans-Olov Adami at Karolinska Institute, had taken part in a symposium on environmental toxins, "Dioxin 2001," in South Korea. Here, not only had he thrown suspicion on the research on dioxins that Lennart Hardell is conducting, but also on other research in the field that had produced alarming results.

Shortly after I had interviewed Lennart Hardell a Swedish paper, *Aftonbladet*, revealed that Hans-Olov Adami's participation in the symposium in South Korea had been entirely funded by an American firm of consultants, Exponent Inc., which, according to the newspaper, "makes use of researchers who question cancer alarms so that industry can continue without interruption". Exponent's clients include the oil industry, chemical companies, and General Motors. Hans-Olov Adami is a member of the committee that selects Nobel Prize Winners in Medicine. One of Exponent's executives, Jack Mandel, had commissioned a report entitled *Dioxin and Cancer*, from Adami. The newspapers says that this report "is to be used by the trade association of the American chlorine industries to convince American environmental authorities that it is not necessary to classify dioxins as carcinogenic". It was said that publication is imminent in the American Chemical Industry's trade journal, *Regulatory Toxicology and Pharmacology*. A document that *Aftonbladet* had unearthed also showed that Hans-Olov Adami had been in contact with the American chemical company, Dow Chemicals. Considering the Swedish Cancer Society's lack of interest in environmental toxins, it is interesting to note that Hans-Olov Adami's professorship in Medical Epidemiology at the Karolinska Institute is funded by the Society. Hans-Olov Adami has denied that he allows his contacts with industry to influence the results of his research. One comment he made to *Aftonbladet*'s journalist was: "Nearly all leading researchers have similar kinds of cooperation. Industry finances research. Everyone realizes that this is just the beginning and that these boundaries will be erased."

In actual fact Adami has made a major contribution to revolutionary changes that have taken place at the Karolinsksa Institute in recent years – changes leading to an ever-increasing number of ties with industry. According to a September 2001 article in *Science*, the Institute encourages its researchers to go into business themselves.

By writing the aforementioned debate article, Hans-Olov Adami and his fellow professors wanted to dissuade the mass media from publishing research findings before they had been given "scientific acceptance." More and more Swedish and international researchers seem to have become tired of these rules for what is suitable in academic spheres, releasing their results to the general public when they feel that the risks need to become quickly known.

10
Microwaves I:
Mobile phones – a worldwide experiment with the blood–brain barrier?

In repeated studies over almost a decade, three professors at Lund University, Sweden, have shown that microwaves, similar to those in mobile phones, open the blood–brain barrier of rats so that proteins carrying poisons can enter the brain. The researchers claim that there is good reason to assume that the same happens in the human brain.

In a lecture given to the European Parliament in June 2000, one of them, neurosurgeon Leif Salford stated:

> The world's largest biological experiment ever, has been taking place for a few years, and soon one quarter of the world's population will be included as test persons in the experiment, voluntarily exposing their brains to electromagnetic fields produced by their mobile phones. The other three quarters constitute a control group, however not ideal, as many of the non-users are exposed to "passive mobile phoning" and other types of radio frequency radiation.

Leif Salford has expressed this warning time and time again during recent years. He and his colleagues, Professors Bertil Persson, radiation physicist, and Arne Brun, neuropathologist, have, in repeated studies over almost a decade, shown that radio frequency electromagnetic fields open the blood–brain barrier of rats so that large proteins, which may carry poisons, can enter the brain. They have confirmed their findings in follow-up studies with real GSM-900 and GSM-1 800 exposures. They have made no bones about the fact that the blood–brain barrier in humans, with the highest probability, reacts in the same way as that of rats.

It wasn't until the end of the 1990s that the results of this research were noticed by journalists. And yet, the three professors had published this news in scientific journals many years earlier, the first report as early as in 1992, and they had also given presentations of their results at various international conferences. They have in no way kept quiet about what they have observed. In a world in which increasing numbers of people are using mobile phones they have felt obliged to tell of their findings even outside the research community. As Bertil Persson expressed it in a Swedish TV program: "We don't want anyone in the future to blame us for not telling about what we have noticed."

There can be no doubt that they have sown fear in the mobile telephony industry. In March 1994, Arvid Brandberg, head of the Swedish telecommunications industry trade group, urged Leif Salford to call George Carlo, who at that time was the leader of a research project on health risks from mobile phones, financed by the Cellular Telecommunications Industry Association, CTIA. It was an early March morning in Washington when Leif Salford's call came, George Carlo tells us in his book *Cellphones, Invisible Hazards in the Wireless Age*, published in January 2001. Leif Salford told George Carlo that he and his colleagues in Lund had studied the effects of microwaves on the brain for several years and were now convinced that they had found a potentially harmful effect. They had consistently observed a breakdown of the blood–brain barrier, following exposures to frequencies that are the same as those from mobile phones.

In his book George Carlo writes that, before beginning to work in the mobile telephony sector, he had studied the effects of chemicals on humans. With herbicides and pesticides as a starting-point he knew how important the blood–brain barrier is and that brain tissues are extremely sensitive to trauma from physical and chemical insult. The barrier is the special "filter" that keeps dangerous chemicals from reaching the brain: "If it were shown that exposure to the radiation from a wireless phone antenna causes a breakdown in this very important defense mechanism, this would be a serious problem," he writes, and continues: "In turn, this could constitute an indirect mechanism for the development of brain cancer – with the radio frequency (RFR) not causing brain cancer directly, but providing a pathway for other cancer-causing chemicals to damage the sensitive brain tissue that would otherwise be protected."

Other researchers had earlier observed effects on the blood–brain barrier caused by electromagnetic radiation, but this was a series of repeated experiments using extremely sensitive methods. George Carlo realized the seriousness of the findings and, shortly after the telephone call, traveled to Stockholm to meet Leif Salford.

Although George Carlo fully understood what these findings meant, remarkably enough he didn't channel any funding to this research whilst he had powers of allocation. Over the years, many bitter researchers have accused him of holding back projects that could be to the disadvantage of the mobile telephony industry. But, at the end of the 1990s it was time for George Carlo to break with CTIA, as he recalls in his book.

Even though no funding was forthcoming from CTIA there are many who have shown great interest in the results produced in the small university city of Lund, close to the south coast of Sweden. American researchers, commissioned by the US Air Force, have been to Lund and conducted preliminary experiments in the Lund researchers' laboratory. They are reproducing the experiments in the Air Force Research Laboratory at Brooks Air Force Base in San Antonio under the leadership of Dr. Michael R. Murphy, whilst in Lund, Salford, Persson, and Brun are continuing to study the possible long-term effects involved.

One of the reasons that Americans have taken interest is the chronic sickness symptoms that have affected thousands of American soldiers after the Gulf War, the first really highly technological war. There are suspicions that the microwaves the soldiers were constantly surrounded by might have caused them injury via this mechanism – if their blood–brain barriers were opened, medicines and other substances from their blood may have entered their brains. The soldiers had been given pyridostigminbromide, an antidote for sarin, a nerve gas, as well as a number of other medicines and vaccines.

The Americans have signed an agreement with the researchers in Lund, concerning collaboration about this question. The intention is to investigate if substances including pyridostigminbromide can leak into the brain via the blood–brain barrier.

Salford, Persson, and Brun have carried out a series of experiments to find out if the blood–brain barrier in rats is affected by static magnetic fields, low frequency pulsed magnetic fields, and radio frequency electromagnetic fields in the microwave range. They have also studied combinations of the three types of fields used for NMR (NeuroMagnetic Resonance) imaging. At an early stage, they found that the exposure to all these fields induced various degrees of leakage of proteins that normally do not pass through the blood–brain barrier. But the effects are strongest when using mobile telephony frequencies.

Other researchers have studied the effects on the blood–brain barrier, but the research group at Lund University were first to use immunohistochemical methods, which permit the identification of even a minor leakage of proteins and give an exact histological localization of this leakage. Experiments have been carried out on larger series, up to 1700 animals, whilst some other researchers in the field have restricted trials to 30 animals, sub-divided into three groups.

The researchers in Lund have repeated their experiments using real mobile phones and have obtained consistent results. The 900 megahertz microwaves from GSM phones, as well as the 1800 megahertz frequencies, cause the brain's protective barrier to let albumin, a protein normally found in the bloodstream, enter the brain. The effect was the same after a few minutes radiation as after a longer period of time. It also occurred at such extremely low energy levels as 0.0004–0.001 W/kg. The SAR value – referred to by the industry – is 2 W/kg. SAR value is the Specific Absorption Rate, the amount of energy from an antenna that passes through a biological tissue during a specific time period. It is measured in watts per kilogram of tissue. "The most remarkable observation in our studies is the fact that SAR values around 1 mW/kg (0.001 W/kg) give rise to a more pronounced albumin leakage than higher SAR values," Leif Salford said in his speech to the European Parliament.

> If the reversed situation were at hand, we feel that the risk from cellular phones, base stations, and other radio frequency emitting sources could be managed by reduction of their emitted energy. The situation that the weakest fields, according to our findings, are the biologically most effective, poses a major problem. The most pronounced blood–brain barrier opening effect of the cellular phone may not be in the most superficial layers of the brain, but several centimeters deep in central cerebral structures.

He added that it could not be excluded that non-users, in the vicinity of cellular phone users, may be influenced by these weak effects.

The Lund researchers use the expression "passive mobile phoning," because they have found that even at a distance of 1.8 meters away from the antenna, there is a SAR value exceeding the lowest one that opens the blood–brain barrier in rats. But, when I interviewed him, Leif Salford pointed out that the thicker skin, muscle, and skull of the human head should be considered.

"Guessing, it may be at a meter from a mobile phone that there is still enough energy left to enable penetration of the human skull and open the blood–brain barrier."

The blood–brain barrier shows a significant opening at values as low as 0.0004 W/kg. The SAR value 2 W/kg, which the authorities in most countries refer to, shows itself, of course, to be totally irrelevant. This maximum permissible value has only been set for thermal effects, i.e. heating, but for a long time researchers have been discussing levels far below that at which thermal effects occur. In unison, the mobile telephony industry and authorities have tried to reassure the general public that radiation from cellular phones "is well below the maximum permissible value" of 2 watt/kg.

If the cells that form the barrier let through albumin, a relatively large protein, we may assume that smaller and equally large proteins from the bloodstream can penetrate into brain tissues. Most of the proteins function as carriers of various substances, including iron. When different poisons enter the blood they immediately bond to some form of transporting protein. Even albumin itself is dangerous for the brain. When albumin has been injected directly into the brains of rats even low doses have caused damage. These doses, insignificantly higher than those observed as penetrating the blood–brain barrier during exposure to microwaves, were sufficient to kill the nerve cells of rats.

But can all this be true for human brains? Yes, says Leif Salford. He has repeated this in public many times: the brain physiology of rats is directly comparable to that of humans. There is extremely good reason to assume that exactly the same happens in the brain of a human when talking on a mobile phone. He mentions that there are parts of the brain that have an area with an open blood–brain barrier where the brain "samples" what is present in the blood. "Here, a small amount of protein usually leaks in, but when proteins begin to seep into the cerebrum as well as other parts of the brain, one can do nothing other than feel worried."

This isn't the first time that the effects of microwaves on the blood–brain barrier have been reported. As early as the 1970s studies were published showing this effect at a frequency of 1300 megahertz and extremely low SAR values, even lower than those reported by the researchers in Lund. In Leif Salford's opinion this could be what is referred to as a "window" effect: "It may even be that weak energy levels have a better chance to influence, as they are equivalent to those of the living organism."

What does this mean for all of us in the present chemical-filled microwave society?

Leif Salford's colleague, Professor Emeritus Arne Brun, a neuropathologist who is still active as a researcher, doesn't deny that he is concerned:

> The blood–brain barrier is, of course, meant to protect the brain. That it can be opened by microwaves is clearly an abnormal circumstance. Numerous substances that are normally not present in the brain may seep in and are potentially harmful.
>
> We don't know yet if this actually happens, but theoretically they could bond with brain myelin, a fatty substance whose function is to provide insulation around nerve fibers and to supply electrical signals around the body. Conductivity worsens in nerve fibers in which the myelin is affected. If brain myelin gets damaged, so that it becomes foreign to its normal environment, the body may react abnormally and begin to break it down.
>
> If the brain reacts to the foreign substances by creating antibodies a major risk arises, as these antibodies, via what we refer to as an autoimmune reaction, could attack brain tissues. Illnesses like MS, Parkinson's disease and early ageing are possible developments over time. The effects may come later. It takes a long time before injury to the nervous system results in symptoms. Humans have a very large reserve capacity.

People in the mobile telephony industry wish to wave these risks aside, saying that the issue of the blood–brain barrier is nothing to worry about, that it also opens due, for example, to high blood pressure?

> Yes, it can be opened by peaks of high blood pressure; it is then a matter of clearly unhealthy levels. The barrier is also opened during epileptic attacks and after severe trauma to the skull.

Does the albumin clear away the poisons it transports when it gets into the brain?

> One might think so, but we haven't been able to prove it. There is no longer any reason for the albumin to retain its content since its function as a carrier is, one might say, completed. It is no longer in its original environment and loses its orientation. Normally, of course, albumin carries poisons to the kidneys and secretes them there.

The blood–brain barrier presumably closes very shortly after exposure to radiation ceases. But it has been observed that albumin remains in the brains of rats for a few days after they have been exposed to radiation. In other experiments with mice roughly the same amounts of albumin have been shown to be able to cause damage to brain cells.

Albumin is a protein that also binds water. If it runs out into tissues it can, therefore, lead to edemas, fluid-filled swellings. Arne Brun describes the acute injuries that he has seen under a microscope as spots around the blood vessels.

> The spots are albumin and antibodies to albumin. We added the antibodies ourselves as a means of identifying the albumin. It's a very sensitive and sure method to be able to identify the albumin.
>
> A little zone around these spots is affected, but outside these

zones we have not been able to observe any damage. Leaks in the blood–brain barrier have, however, occurred in rather many places so a certain proportion of the tissue is damaged.

A question that a lot of people are asking is if this mechanism could be the cause of acute symptoms that many experience when close to electronic devices. If the blood–brain barrier opens, is it conceivable that one might feel it?

> Yes, I think it is possible if some poison, which happens to be present in the blood of an individual at the time, is released. This is speculation, but it is conceivable. We haven't tested the cognitive ability of the rats, or their ability to orient themselves, but we have planned to do so to look for possible temporary disturbances.

Maybe they get something similar to the "radio operator sickness" that was talked about in the 1930s? But you can't really say that rats have psychosomatic problems, which was the way the doctors wanted to use in explaining that sickness? "They'll certainly try to," says Arne Brun with a smile.

There is no mistaking that Arne Brun views the new technological advances, such as smart homes "where we communicate with our fridges" and live in an ocean of microwaves, as risky. So, he and his colleagues are continuing their research, even if it isn't especially sought after. Financial allocations are parsimonious. As a matter of fact, this research group had not been allocated any EU funding when I interviewed them. The European mobile telephony industry channels its research contributions to the EU, but how this funding is utilized is another story. RALF, the Swedish Council for Working Life Research, has also exhibited a great lack of interest in this field. "But we aren't going to give up because we don't get much funding," says Leif Salford, referring to his own "professor's salary" and that of his colleagues. "We can't work at top speed, but we plod on."

Both a German and a French group of researchers have shown the same kind of effects.

A great deal has been written about the "three giants" in the sector, Nokia, Ericsson, and Motorola, having developed and even applied for patents for radiation shields in their cellular phones. It is said that this development has taken place since 1993. If true it appears to have happened at the same time that the three researchers in Lund began to observe alarming effects. But, outwardly, the industry in alliance with the authorities has kept a straight face.

In the debate about cell phone radiation the risks from radiation have most commonly been linked with brain tumors and other forms of cancer. The possible neurological effects have been overshadowed. But it is from this field that research results have frightened the industry most of all.

The first time I interviewed Veli Santonmaa, who, until recently, held responsibility for research questions at Nokia in Finland, he waved aside all the alarming studies that I mentioned, but to a question about the researchers at Lund University he let slip, "yes, that's something one has to take seriously". The next time I called him, however, he complied with the general policy of the mobile telephony industry and explained that "we have come to the conclusion that this is a question of an artifact". An artifact is a mistake, not a genuine but a curious side effect of research.

But the same results in repeated studies over a ten-year period, using advanced research methods, isn't something to be brushed aside, using the explanation that it is a question of an artifact. Nor can one make a joke of it, as a Swedish representative of the industry tried to do at a conference, "you all know, of course, that the blood–brain barrier is opened by a little alcohol?"

The mobile telephony sector likes to use the term "radio frequencies" for microwaves. "We usually avoid using the word microwaves as it scares people," as one representative of the

Swedish mobile telephony industry let slip in an information meeting. Incidentally, in a report to the Swedish Government, known as the RALF Report, written in December 2000, the following description is to be found "radio frequency fields in the frequency range 0.9–2.8 gigahertz." It isn't exactly the first thing that comes to mind that 0.9 gigahertz is the same as 900 megahertz, the frequency emitted by GSM cell phones; microwaves start as low as 300 megahertz.

In 2003 the mobile telephony industry's remarks about artifacts in connection with the findings of the Lund researchers came to an abrupt end when it became known that they had also found damage to nerve cells in brain after exposure to microwaves from GSM mobile phones. After having repeatedly demonstrated that weak pulsed microwaves give rise to significant leakage of albumin through the blood–brain barrier they had gone on to investigate if this pathological leakage might be combined with damage to neurons. They had exposed three different groups each of 8 rats to GSM mobile phone electromagnetic fields of different strengths for two hours. In the journal *Environmental Health* they wrote: "We found, and present here for the first time, highly significant ($p< 0.002$) evidence for neuronal damage in both the cortex, the hippocampus, and the basal ganglia in the brains of exposed rats."

They explained their use of 12 to 26 week old rats in the experiment by saying "they are comparable to human mobile phone addicted teenagers with respect to age". They meant that we ought to treat these risks seriously, especially those to young people's brains:

> A neuronal damage of the kind here described, may not have immediately demonstrable consequences, even if repeated. It may, however, in the long run, result in reduced brain reserve capacity that might be unveiled by other later neuronal decreases

or even the wear and tear of ageing. We cannot exclude that after some decades of (often) daily use, a whole generation of users may suffer negative effects, maybe as soon as in their middle age.

11

Microwaves II: Ericsson's denial

In 1991 the Ericsson subsidiary, Ellemtel, got the largest state working environment grant ever to have been allocated in Sweden. A Working Life Fund, created on the initiative of Anna-Greta Leijon, the Minister of Labor at that time, provided 8.9 million Swedish crowns (US$ 1 million) for measures needed when around 60 engineers at the company had developed electro-hypersensitivity.

Ten years later, the company, now named Ericsson AXE Research and Development, didn't want to hear about electro-hypersensitivity. They have fired Per Segerbäck, the most severely afflicted designer, using his disability as the sole motivation. Other persons with the same type of symptoms in the company have been silenced. It all started in 1987 when Ellemtel, then owned by Ericsson and Telia (the latter the national telephone operator in Sweden – today it is the largest cellular operator), had problems with electro-hypersensitivity among its employees. This happened to coincide with the installation of a base station for mobile telephony for the Scandinavian analogue systems NMT 450 and NMT 900 on the roof of the company building. The transmitters were brought into service between November 1987 and January 1988. Many are certain that it was not by chance that this was when the problems started. Inside the building, the future of Ericsson, their young designers, were busy working in front of their vdus. At this time, Ellemtel had the highest "computer density" of all companies in Sweden at 2.5 screens per designer. The designers were now exposed to different kinds of electromagnetic radiation, different frequencies from the vdus and other electronic equipment, and microwaves from the base station antennas less than 50 meters from their desks. The health effects of this type of mixed exposure are as yet unknown.

However, we must not forget one important additional factor: The designers were also exposed to numerous chemicals. There was not only the constant emissions from the plastic casings and electronics inside all the equipment, the employees were also in direct contact with different electronic components used in building and testing prototypes. When soldering, the chemical emissions can increase by several hundred per cent, due to the heat of the soldering process. The capability of the printed circuit boards in handling electric current was tested by increasing the current until the copper foil interconnections "fused" – with smelly boiling and burning boards as the result. The designers were exposed to these toxic fumes without protection of any kind.

In the 1970s and up to the beginning of the 1980s, Per Segerbäck handled numerous boards and toxic chemicals in his work. He designed and built prototypes – cutting and soldering the circuit boards. He also made measurements on the designs, documenting oscilloscope graphs with a special camera, using a noxious development "gel" and a fixative fluid. He remembers that the smelly chemicals gave him nausea.

Printed circuit boards usually consist of a glass fiber laminated epoxy plastic substrate, with several layers of copper for power supply and interconnections. Various components are mounted on the surface. Most of the time, some epoxy that is not fully hardened is left in the products. When this "soft" epoxy is broken down by heating, for example from soldering, it generates a large number of chemicals, including isocyanates. In the components there are flame-retardant substances such as Tetrabromobisphenol-A, tbbpa. In reality, flame-retardants can only withstand what corresponds to the heat of a glowing cigarette. In a fire, they actually make things worse by producing poisonous gases.

In a Swedish report from 1991 about the phasing out of lead and brominated flame-retardants, written by Per Hedemalm and published by the Swedish Institute of Production Engineering Research, it is stated that printed circuit boards should not be touched with bare hands. In order to avoid damage to the boards, gloves should be used because of the corrosive nature of sweat. Furthermore, people who handle printed circuit boards should take precautions for their own sakes.

Did Ericsson's subsidiary follow rules like this? No – no one knew about the nature of the chemicals they were exposed to. Employees were working in ordinary offices with poor ventilation, without gloves, facemasks, or dedicated evacuation vents. An engineer who worked at Ellemtel at the end of the 1980s is highly critical of the working environment: "I have never felt such discomfort in front of a computer screen as I felt there. You could always feel the smell of chemicals."

By 1985, the Canadian work environment expert, Bob DeMatteo, had written about synergistic effects between different kinds of radiation and between radiation and chemicals in his book *Terminal Shock*. I quote:

> Similarly, the effects of radiation may be enhanced when exposure occurs together with other factors. The simultaneous exposure to several kinds of radiation at the same time will have greater biological effect than when each form of radiation acts independently.

He also writes:

> A reinforcing of the biological effect also has been found for successive exposure to radio frequency fields and ultraviolet radiation. Radio frequency fields can also affect the known actions of certain chemical substances on the body.

It might have been expected that aspects of this kind would have been brought to light when the Swedish State so generously provided Ellemtel with taxpayers' money. But this was not to be. The problems at Ellemtel continued to increase during the period 1989–1990. Within one month 13 engineers became sick. Their symptoms were burning sensations in their faces and on other parts of their bodies. They complained of nausea and dizziness. Some of them could not stand the working environment, but had to take sick leave. The total number of cases was now around 50. Later, more cases showed up, but as the official line changed from openness to total silence, the exact number is unknown. This happened after Lars Ramqvist, at that time the Chairman of the Board for the Ericsson Group, stated: "We have no problems with electro-hypersensitivity at Ericsson."

When the problems were present at Ellemtel, at the end of the 1980s, the company turned to Associate Professor Yngve Hamnerius of Chalmers, Gothenburg, and Stockholm Energy, which had wide experience in minimizing electromagnetic fields from transformers and other equipment. Among many other specialties, they offered a fully welded aluminum cage with extremely good low-frequency shielding characteristics. A complete "electrical sanitization" was performed; encapsulation, screening, etc. took place, all this to good effect. The afflicted employees could return to work.

Per Segerbäck, the manager of a team in which almost everybody became electro-hypersensitive, now got a special room with double shields; on the outside two layers of "transformer" plates, completely covered with a welded layer of 5 mm aluminum on the inside. Ericsson had previously performed similar shielding and "sanitization" in his home. Altogether, the company had spent four million Swedish crowns on measures for these fifty employees, the payoff being they could go back to work.

But now a whole new phase started with the appearance of a consultant, named Mats Frånberg. On Ellemtel's behalf Mats Frånberg applied for funds from the aforementioned Working

Life Fund. As he stated in the application, the company wanted to "try out, consolidate, gain approval for, and generalize" what had been achieved in the "internal project." He emphasized that it had been concluded that electromagnetic fields had been a factor of importance when the engineers had developed their illnesses.

One can assume that the Working Life Fund had great expectations that Ellemtel would clarify the cause of electro-hypersensitivity, for the good of all companies and employees in the country who had been struck by this malady. There is no other explanation for the decision by the Fund to allow an amount as large as US $ 1 million and to, against normal practice, pay it in advance, before the new project had even started.

Now, Mats Frånberg's period of greatness as a consultant project manager began. Within the company there was not very much for him to do because Yngve Hamnerius and Stockholm Energy had already solved the practical problems. Though not cured of their hypersensitivity, the employees could work. However, an inventive consultant can always generate activities. Mats Frånberg now gathered a team of researchers, all with the common view that the cure for electro-hypersensitive people is cognitive therapy, acupuncture, and similar measures. One of the leading promoters of cognitive therapy for this type of illness was Professor Sture Lidén at Karolinska Hospital. He was often seen in the corridors of Ellemtel but never even bothered to meet Per Segerbäck. "I do not think he ever spoke to any of those afflicted by electro-hypersensitivity at the company," says Per Segerbäck.

Mats Frånberg helped the researchers in the network to apply for more money from other funds in Sweden. He also made contact with all of the authorities and organizations involved in the electro-hypersensitivity issue and began to manipulate them in a manner that was not obvious until much later.

It became common knowledge at various workplaces in Sweden that if you wanted to apply for funding from the Working Life Fund for projects concerning electro-hypersensitivity you should "go via Ellemtel." Sometimes Mats Frånberg offered to put a word in for other applicants, but then often made it clear that some of the funding should go to Ellemtel. He had gained support for the application from Ellemtel within the Central Working Life Fund, which managed several regional funds. At the same time, he got the Fund to sign an agreement that Ellemtel, that is Mats Frånberg, should be heard before the Fund awarded any new funding for projects of this kind. In other words, he was a referee for the fund.

How could the management of the Fund be so credulous? The answer might be that no one really knew what ought to be done to solve this new working environment problem and that Mats Frånberg was purposeful and enterprising. The climate was right for an inventive consultant. In the Regional Fund for the County of Stockholm, which was officially in charge of controlling the project of Ellemtel, no one had any idea what needed to be checked. The whole problem complex was new and unknown. So, it isn't surprising that the manager of the Fund agreed to classify all material from the Ellemtel project as secret for some time. Probably the secrecy classification was ordered by Mats Frånberg to stop journalists finding out that the entire project was mostly air. The only documents that had been sent to the Fund were some insignificant brochures and pamphlets, Frånberg's business card and a number of bombastic letters from him to various authorities; I discovered this when I managed to have the secrecy classification broken. There was also a report stating that some of the electro-hypersensitive employees in the company were of the opinion that acupuncture improved their condition. The authors of this acupuncture report were the skin specialist Mats Berg, mentioned earlier, and a stress researcher Bengt Arnetz, who had not asked for their study to become classified as secret information. When assessed using criteria suitable for government-sponsored research, their report was, of course, embarrassingly simple.

Now, Ericsson, a private enterprise, was in full control of practically all research and projects related to hypersensitivity to electromagnetic fields. Most people had lost interest by the time the final report from Ellemtel was published in 1993. The employers and individuals around the country, who had been hoping for assistance from Ellemtel, had become disappointed because of all the secrecy. The press conference attracted only a few journalists. This, the most expensive Swedish project report ever on electro-hypersensitivity, contained nothing new. Everything with some substance in the report was already known to the initiated. The rest was idle talk.

Per Segerbäck is very critical of Bengt Arnetz, who, he thinks, did great and irreparable damage to all those who suffer from electro-hypersensitivity.

> He made a thorough investigation of our stress levels and presented results to us showing that the part of the staff that had electro-hypersensitivity problems actually had less stress problems than the control group. However, he never published these findings.
>
> But he kept on talking about "techno-stress," for which he did not have any proof, at least not at Ellemtel.

You might have expected the Ellemtel project to look into the issue of chemical influence: what chemicals are used in electronic equipment; what health effects may they have in the long term; what are the combined effects of chemicals and electromagnetic fields; what research is needed?

Nevertheless, Ellemtel was content with a small literature review produced by an employee at the National Board of Housing, Building, and Planning. When I asked why chemicals were not given more cover, Mats Frånberg answered that he "found the Board of Housing, Building, and Planning at too late a stage". While the project was going on I regularly called Mats Frånberg and asked him "how far have you come with the issue of chemicals?" Just as regularly, he replied: "We will report that soon enough." He never gave any interviews during the project period.

Today, Ericsson is contacting one chemist after another at

Swedish universities in order to analyze and measure the chemicals used in mobile phones. According to my information, when researchers agree to cooperate, they promise not to publish their findings.

Per Segerbäck, an expert on integrated circuit designs, was 37 years old when the "Mats Frånberg era" at Ellemtel ended. He had not seen much of the costly project; his only interest was his job. He was somewhat of a workaholic. That was his unlucky fate. He had traveled the world for Ericsson and he had worked on microprocessor design at Advanced Micro Devices in Silicon Valley in California. He had brought powerful workstations to Ericsson for design work. Now, he was confined in two shielded rooms, one at the Ellemtel office, one at home. He went between these two places in an old diesel-powered Mercedes taxi, tolerable due to its lack of ignition system and modern electronics.

Why did he get so severely afflicted? The main reason is, maybe, that he paid no attention to the danger signals for as long as possible. This is his story: He became ill at the end of 1988. Towards weekends he started getting a stinging and burning sensation in his skin. During Saturdays and Sundays the situation improved. He used to prefer having all the fluorescent lamps in the office on, now he found he couldn't tolerate them. Others in his team started complaining about similar symptoms, especially those who, like himself, worked overtime in the evenings. It was very common for the designers at Ellemtel to work overtime. It went so far that the company introduced a rule in 1990 that no one was allowed to work between midnight and six in the morning.

In summer 1989, Per Segerbäck had developed hypersensitivity to both electricity and light. On holiday that summer he found he couldn't even buy ice cream for his children in a small shop, due to the fluorescent lights. In January 1990 the situation was critical. Per Segerbäck could neither stand the environment in the office, nor at home. He called in sick, but had no place to go. In the middle of the winter he slept in his car. Several other employees at Ellemtel were on sick leave with similar symptoms, but Per Segerbäck seemed to be the most severely afflicted. Several times he had serious heart attacks. It was at this stage that Yngve Hamnerius was called upon to give advice on how to carry out electrical sanitization, first in Per Segerbäck's home, then at Ellemtel.

During 1991 Per Segerbäck went back to work, at first in a large van, void of electrical installations, then into the shielded room where he could work with a special low radiation, Ellemtel-designed, LCD-monitor. Close to his room were the offices of his electro-hypersensitive colleagues.

After almost a year of sick leave, Per Segerbäck was back at work. He still had symptoms, but the important thing was that he could continue working. Everything seemed to be working out fine. That was until the extremely rapid expansion of the digital GSM cellular phone system took place in 1997. Within a few months it became impossible for him to tolerate traveling to the Ellemtel office, now called Ericsson AXE Research and Development. He had to do all his work from home. In spite of these problems, his managers were very satisfied with his performance. But, what now made things even worse was that the cellular operator Comviq/ Tele 2 installed a base station only two hundred meters from his home, which was also his office.

In January 1999, two days before the station was to be put into regular service, Per Segerbäck had to be rushed from his home to a camper about forty kilometers away on Lovön Island. This is just a few kilometers from Drottningholm castle, where the Swedish Royal Family lives. Due to the microwave exposure along the way, Per Segerbäck was unconscious when his relatives moved him out of the car into the camping van, they told me later.

The environment on Lovön Island was very good for Per Segerbäck, though the camper was cramped and cold. One of his qualities is that he always gets back to work as soon as he can. He did so this time, too. He soon found out that there was space available in a nearby building that belonged to the Geological Survey of Sweden and that it was possible to rent one of the rooms. But his employer didn't want to have anything to do with such a solution.

Then Per Segerbäck found a derelict shed belonging to a local farmer and was allowed to use it. "Ericsson AXE Research and Development," he answered when people phoned him at the old barn, now storage space for all sorts of junk. The only creatures seen around him were hens, peacefully picking outside. He set up his electro-sanitized VDU amidst all the junk and, at a safe distance, the computer. He had an electro-sanitized telephone beside the screen. These were the only items of modern technology. Everything else was inside Per Segerbäck's head. Working as long as daylight allowed, he continued to develop the AXE-system, in contact with colleagues via e-mail and the Internet.

It was an unbelievable working environment for anyone; it was even more astonishing to find it being used by an Ericsson employee. But Per Segerbäck wasn't interested in sensationalism; he wanted to get on with his work. He had never been one to give up in the face of difficulties. He has a strong sense of duty and was interested in the work he was doing. He didn't seem to care about his surroundings. But storm clouds were on the horizon. Rumors about his "office" had spread in the company. Different employer's representatives had been out to pay Per Segerbäck a visit and had been shocked. Some of them were probably scared that some inspector of works might find out that Ericsson was not complying with working environment laws.

Many of the managers and foremen that had worked in Ellemtel had left. New ones had been taken on in the new company and they didn't know much about what had happened at the beginning of the 1990s. Shortly after finishing off the major Ellemtel project the personnel who were electro-hypersensitive had been dispersed throughout the organization. No one dared to object when it was explained that electro-hypersensitivity was no longer a problem.

Now, negative signals began to come from the employer, starting with a suggestion that Per Segerbäck ought to consider taking a disability pension. He said "no." Then the company asked if he could consider starting his own company and continuing to work as a consultant to Ericsson. It was not a very attractive offer. Of course it was possible to carry out design work at a distance, but how do you sell your services as a consultant to clients when you can't tolerate their working environment?

In July 1999 Per Segerbäck found a house in the forests some miles north of Stockholm. Here he could work in entirely different surroundings, in an environment that enabled him to view the future with some degree of confidence. But the harassment from Ericsson grew in strength. Now they refused to offer him any kind of work at all. They demanded that he should be at the main office for all his working time. But they made it impossible for him to be there. He was no longer allowed to use the room that Yngve Hamnerius and Stockholm Energy had put in order for him. He would be obliged to use a normal room.

Things began to happen rapidly. Despite strong protests from his union and negotiations with the employer it all ended in Per Segerbäck being served notice of termination of employment on 25 October 1999.

In November 2000 a unique trial took place in a tiny church hall in Hallstavik, not far from the cottage Per Segerbäck lives in. His trade union, the Swedish Union of Clerical and Technical Employees, SIF, had charged Ericsson AXE Research Development of unlawful termination of employment. The proceedings were handled by the Labor Court, at which the employer was represented by a lawyer from a powerful employers' association.

Per Segerbäck's severe hypersensitivity was the reason for holding proceedings in such pastoral surroundings. Under normal circumstances the Labor Court is convened in Stockholm's Old Town. Per Segerbäck came to the proceedings dressed in a protection suit of the type worn by German and American workers in the microwave industry. He also had a visor in front of his face, to protect him from radiation. The media reacted as expected, writing more about the protection suit – referred to as a "space suit" – than about the actual proceedings, thus creating a favorable situation for the employer's lawyer, who wanted to paint a picture of someone who was unable to do any kind of work because of his hypersensitivity.

SIF's lawyer had informed the Labor Court that she wanted to submit an application for the case to be tried under a new law, prohibiting discrimination at workplaces against persons with a functional disorder. At the last moment it was discovered that the law referred only to those seeking employment, not those already employed. Thus only the Security of Employment Act was applicable. SIF lost the case. The Court ruled entirely in favor of Ericsson. This was a terrible blow for Per Segerbäck and all those who find themselves in similar circumstances. This precedent shows how insecure the situation is for those who are afflicted by ill health. But the ruling should also have given unions reason to examine themselves, perhaps above all looking at their own magazines. Per Segerbäck's own union journal had shown the least possible interest for his case and had never thrown light on the underlying circumstances in an understandable manner.

There is also good reason for the mass media as a whole to be self-critical. They described this remarkable trial in which the members of the Labor Court, Per Segerbäck, and others attending the sessions sat in November darkness, a darkness lit up only by candles, in a very one-sided way. Not one journalist even mentioned that Ericsson had been given almost 9 million crowns by the state to take steps so that their electro-hypersensitive technicians could continue working for them. No one reported that it was something in the work environment that had given rise to Per Segerbäck's illness. Not one word was written about a working environment filled with chemicals and subjected to microwaves from the company's roof. Instead, misinformation was spread by the media about how the employer had spent millions for Per Segerbäck's sake.

The truth was that the initial 4 million crowns spent on electro-sanitization was not only for Per Segerbäck, but also for other employees. Thereafter, no special measures were taken by the company to help Per Segerbäck to continue working. He never saw a penny of all the millions that were given to Ericsson by the Swedish state. He didn't even get any use from the measures provided via this funding – the truth is that no one can really say for certain if any measures that helped those afflicted were ever taken. But Per Segerbäck had continued to work without help, despite his severe handicap, which he began to suffer because of the work environment at an Ericsson company.

Ericsson was never exposed to the troublesome questions about what they had achieved using state funding and why they never mentioned chemicals and microwaves which, as far as it is possible to ascertain, made Per Segerbäck ill. It is difficult for journalists to understand what it is all about. Chief editors don't want to allocate resources to penetrating journalism in this controversial area and many journalists are reluctant to write about the subject.

There are several reasons for talking about David and Goliath. Per Segerbäck didn't just lose in the Labor Court, he also lost severance pay that he ought to have been entitled to. But what he felt worst about was that he suddenly lost contact with working life, a contact that he had kept via his electro-sanitized VDU. In autumn 2001 Per Segerbäck was forced to accept a disability pension, a solution that he had tried to avoid as long as possible. For some reason his union failed to see that they had an opportunity to employ Per Segerbäck as a working environment expert in this field.

Why did Ericsson take this drastic step? It had nothing to do with Per Segerbäck's competence and ability to work. The employer has not made one concrete negative comment about these. On the contrary, many in the company can bear witness – and did so in the Labor Court – to his keeping abreast of technological developments despite appalling working conditions. Minutes from negotiations between the union and the employer have been "as thin as postage stamps," says Lars-Erik Sjölund, chairman of SIF's local branch in the company. This implies that the employer did not have any concrete reason for terminating employment. "I find it difficult to understand our employer's actions unless they are meant to frighten others who are hypersensitive to electricity. The aim seems to be that everyone should know that electro-hypersensitivity can lead to losing your job. But Ericsson loses dignity and goodwill by these actions."

One can, naturally, understand that employees in protection suits against microwaves are not the best advertisement for the company's products. The suggestion of a protection suit really came from the union, as a solution when the company demanded that Per Segerbäck must attend meetings in the workplace. The regional social insurance office provided the US $2500 that the suit cost. Ericsson felt they couldn't afford this. But, says Lars-Eric Sjölund, it would have been easy for Ericsson to organize videoconference facilities instead, so that Per Segerbäck could have been at the meetings. "It's within our field to fix such things. It wouldn't have cost that much."

The most probable explanation of the way the company acted is that Per Segerbäck, over the years, has developed into one of the most knowledgeable people in Sweden when it comes to the health hazards of microwaves. He is just too dangerous for Ericsson and the whole cellular phone industry.

12

Microwaves III: Close exposure to microwaves, chemicals, circuit boards, soldering fumes: connection to deteriorating sight denied

Anders Lindström was exposed to both chemicals and microwaves when he tested equipment for mobile phone base stations at Ericsson Radio Systems. His sight became badly impaired but the company has denied that his working conditions could be the cause. Anders Lindström was just a fly in the ointment, an unpleasant reminder that employees' health is the price of progress.

Anders Lindström was 34 when I interviewed him for the first time. Only a few years before, he had been an active sportsman. To keep fit, he used to run 20–30 miles each week, he played tennis and was doing some bodybuilding. Today his sight is badly impaired, he has chronic pains in his eyes and in the skin around them, as well as a large number of other symptoms that no doctor has been able to establish the cause of. He has to stay in his flat almost all the time because of his poor sight.

When working at Ericsson Radio Systems in Gävle, north of Stockholm, he was exposed to both chemicals and microwaves when he tested equipment for mobile telephony base stations. But no one will admit that his problem depend on an occupational injury. "I've lost the best years of my youth. But neither the company nor the union have helped me to get my disability investigated, nor have doctors."

Anders Lindström was employed in 1988. His work consisted

of testing and repairing antenna distributors, units that distribute analogue microwaves in base stations for mobile telephony. He also tested and repaired power amplifiers for GSM transmitters, units that strengthen digital microwaves. Anders Lindström:

> I tested equipment for GSM with covers removed, at a distance of about a foot (30–40 cm). The output produced was around 40 watts, about the same as radiation from 40 cell phones.
> You had to be careful that you didn't burn the tops of your fingers, after about a tenth of a second you began to smell burnt skin.

The units had metal bases on which five printed circuit cards were fixed. Three of the cards were used for amplification. Two of the cards were in direct contact with the cooling flange, which was the size of a brick. A cooling paste had been spread on it to transfer heat efficiently from the cards to the flange. Before he became ill he had no reason to think about what the cooling paste on the flange was made of, or what effects the radiation he was working with could have. It was never talked about. At a much later date he demanded to know the brand name of the paste and have a specification of ingredients.

> I have been told by the person in charge of rehabilitation in the company that the paste was so harmless that it could be used as lip-gloss. However, the product information indicated that skin could peel off if it repeatedly came into contact with the paste. If the ventilation was insufficient, a facemask should be worn. Further, both protective glasses and protective breathing devices were required when soldering.
>
> I had the soldering iron's temperature set at 340 degrees C and my nose right above the fumes that occur when soldering.

Later he found out that soldering wire contains substances that it is necessary to take precautions against. According to the product information he acquired it contains lead, tin, and colophony, sometimes even silver. These substances can cause toxic symptoms if you breathe in fumes from heated products.

> The product information also says that you should immediately go to a doctor if you get breathing difficulties, eye problems, or other reactions. I did so, but at the company's medical care facility I wasn't even able to see a doctor when I had acute problems.

Anders Lindström had worked without any kind of precautionary measures, although it was known that anyone inhaling fumes or dust from this type of soldering wire could get acute toxic effects such as dizziness, headaches, and irritation in the respiratory organs. In the product information it was clearly stated that there was a risk of injuries to the cornea and inflammation of the iris. Anders Lindström had injuries to the cornea. During the whole time that he worked at Ericsson Radio System, from 1988 to 1997, he was exposed both to microwaves and unknown quantities of various chemical emissions.

In 1991 he began to have problems with a congested nose and eye irritation. Three of his colleagues, who were power amplifier testers, also complained about nasal congestion. A doctor advised them to have operations on their noses; bent noses can give rise to nasal congestion, they were told. Anders Lindström was referred to a specialist, who said that his nose was not so bent for an operation to be necessary.

He had begun to have a number of symptoms that doctors couldn't explain. He had bouts of dizziness and felt sick several times a day when at work. At nights he had attacks of what felt like cramp in his lungs and raised blood pressure in his brain, as he explained things. His eyes ached and ran. In the company medical care journals it is noted that he came in for emergency care in 1993 when a body rash broke out whilst he was at work. There are also notes that he had severe asthma-like problems.

After a while his complaints changed to severe pain in and around the eyes. His face swelled up. The company doctor thought that Anders Lindström was allergic to something at work and referred to earlier pollen and fur allergies. Another doctor, at the medical center in Gävle, thought that the cramp attacks were a sign of depression and prescribed Cipramil, an anti-depressive medicine. Anders Lindström: "I took the pills for ten days but stopped because I couldn't sleep."

His liver counts also became high, but he was told it was nothing to worry about. As he didn't drink more than the occasional beer, he wondered what could have caused the raised liver counts. It wasn't until 2001 that they began to fall. In 1995 an optician had noted that he was a little long-sighted but had no other major eye problems. Shortly thereafter, in February 1996, Anders Lindström's sight began to deteriorate rapidly. By July that year both eyes were seriously affected, the right-hand one being worst. At the eye clinic in Gävle County Hospital they were surprised at this rapid deterioration. The diagnosis was keratoconus, a swelling of the cornea, but they weren't really sure. What was puzzling was that such changes usually develop over a period of two to three years. Despite Anders Lindström not having much sight left in his right eye, the specialist in the eye clinic was reluctant to recommend a cornea transplant.

In February 1997 Anders Lindström was put on the sick list full time. He had such severe pain and poor sight that he was unable to do any work at all. He couldn't carry out normal daily activities without assistance. After putting some pressure on, he was finally referred to the Academic Hospital in Uppsala for a cornea transplant. Here they were surprised that the referral hadn't been earlier. In May 1997 they operated on his right eye. At first his sight improved, but relapsed quickly during the autumn. An associate professor at the hospital thought it was just a temporary relapse, but that the eye pains and facial swelling warranted a referral to a neurologist. This opinion was not shared by Anders Lindström's doctor in his home city. At last a doctor at an eye clinic in Gävle wrote a referral to a neurologist. This led to nothing new. The specialist didn't think that the symptoms were caused by neurological injuries, there were no nerves in the face that could give such symptoms, he explained. "I wonder why my family doctor has prescribed acupuncture," Anders Lindström commented.

After having been on the sick list for almost a year, and not having been called to the company health care service for examination, nor having heard from his supervisor at work, Anders Lindström wrote a letter to the local branch of the Metalworkers' Union and one to the regional social insurance office. He asked if they could help him in any way. The social insurance office replied: "What should we do then?" But the union saw to it that he was called to the healthcare service in the company, where he got a referral for computer tomography. This showed that the area around the optic nerve was normal. Heart and lung x-rays revealed nothing unusual either. Anders Lindström felt somewhat relieved, now at least he knew he didn't have a tumor. But the pain and sight impairment still remained.

At the same time as Anders Lindström was fighting desperately to at least have a thorough examination, a local paper in Gävle published an article about an alarm about work environment hazards at Ericsson Radio Systems, raised by a safety officer in the company. He held that employees in the plant could have injuries arising from isocyanates. The symptoms were dry coughs, nasal congestion, eye irritations, and asthma-like attacks, just the same that Anders Lindström had. Eight repairmen had filed a claim for occupational injuries compensation citing skin complaints, according to the newspaper.

An ombudsman from the Swedish Metal Workers' Union had visited the plant and taken measurements. He had said that about 10 employees had signs of being exposed to isocyanates. They had worked on printed circuit cards repairs. The safety officer took vigorous action but, later, he was said to have become awkward and resigned. The debate on isocyanates ebbed out.

Whilst Anders Lindström was working at the plant, no samples were ever taken to check if he had isocyanates in his blood. But the following can be read in the company medical care journals from 1996, his worst period: "... becomes red and has heated face, running eyes, congested nose. These complaints arise as soon as he starts to work. There are a lot of fumes from soldering at work. He gets better in the afternoon when less soldering takes place."

In the same year the company doctor had noted: "The patient is clearly hyper-reactive to soldering fumes." Even so, no thorough examination was carried out. Later, when he wanted to be examined to find out if he had isocyanates in his blood, a doctor said to him that it was completely unnecessary to look for such poisons, "they leave the body after only a few months". The help the doctor could offer was a course in relaxation techniques, so that Anders Lindström could "get to know his face". "I had pains in my skin and eyes before I lost my sight, so I couldn't agree that the pain was caused by the problems with my sight."

At the end of 1997 Anders Lindström raised the question of microwaves. Could he possibly have been injured by a combination of microwaves and chemicals at his workplace? A specialist at the department for occupational and environmental medicine at the University Hospital in Uppsala agreed that it could be possible. He promised to get back to Anders after consultation with colleagues. But nothing happened, except that the specialist changed his opinion. In a letter to Anders Lindström's company doctor he wrote that the eye problem, keratoconus, could not be explained by electromagnetic fields, "nor has there been any exposure to microwaves, which can give rise to thermal injuries". The specialist talks of thermal injuries as the only risk. He seems to have been totally unaware of the fact that the debate during recent years has been about health risks at non-thermal energy levels of microwaves, i.e. energy levels below that at which heat arises. In actual fact the theory that only thermal injuries may be possible is way out of date, even though authorities and industry often refer to it. The recommended limits are based on the level at which opacity is seen in the eye lenses of monkeys.

As the specialist stated that he had searched Medline on the Internet and not found any information on cornea injuries linked to microwaves, Anders Lindström has been helped to run a quick search of Medline by Ragnar Forshufvud, MSc and author. There was quite a lot readily available, including a summary on eyes and microwave radiation from an occupational medicine viewpoint, compiled by the Canadian Center for Occupational Health and Safety in Hamilton, Ontario. This states that microwaves affect the tissues in two ways, either thermally or non-thermally, that is, with or without heat. Microwaves can initiate changes in living tissue at non-thermal levels. In the summary it is especially noted that the cornea can be damaged by microwaves alone, as well as by microwaves combined with certain medicines. Non-thermal injuries from microwaves have been both discussed and reported on since the end of the Second World War. As early as the 1940s it was discovered that there was a risk of cataracts occurring. Short-term animal exposure showed nothing at first, but upon checking after three days, and again after a longer lapse of time, signs of the formation of cataracts were observed.

At the beginning of the 1970s researchers at Rochester University in New York, in a summary of the effects of microwaves on eyes, explained that there was no doubt that cataracts could be developed in animals; concerning the effects on people there was still uncertainty. In 1997, Aurell and Tengroth, two Swedish researchers, reported that they had found a significantly higher number of employees with cataracts at a factory where electrical equipment was tested compared with a control group. In addition, some employees had injuries directly on the retina. In this context, it is interesting that, as early as the 1970s, the Swedish Defense Research Establishment (FOA) had recommended that people who were constantly working with radio frequency radiation of a density of 10 watts per square meter ought to have regular medical examinations. This was especially recommended if unexplained symptoms such as feeling sick, headaches, or visual disorders arose.

Milton Zaret, an American eye specialist, wrote a report on connections between different forms of radiation and eye injuries, including some to the cornea. As early as 1969 a research group that Zaret belonged to had shown that low-frequency electromagnetic fields at 70 Hz could cause injuries on the cornea. Some of the fields in VDUs alternate around 70 Hz. Milton Zaret had also examined lens' alterations in 750 people who had been exposed to microwaves at work, comparing them with a control group of 550 people. His conclusion was that the eye lens could be regarded as a means of measuring the cumulative effects of exposure to microwaves that a human being has been subjected to.

During the 1980s there were reports from Australia and the UK that lens problems were common among radio transmitter and receiver repair workers. That electromagnetic radiation can cause cataracts has been known for many years, wrote Bob DeMatteo, the Canadian work environment expert, in his book *Terminal Shock* in 1986. He pointed out that eyes are very sensitive to radio frequencies and microwaves. The groups of occupations named in this context are pilots, traffic controllers, radio technicians, radio operators, and personnel who use VDUs in offices.

In 1988 the researcher Robert Birge at the Carnegie-Mellon University in the USA found that microwaves with energy levels below the level of heating caused changes in the light-sensitive, chemical substances in the retina. The find was dismissed on the grounds that there was no explanation, no mechanism, for such a non-thermal effect. Data from Birge's research is no longer available, according to Robert O. Becker, the American doctor and researcher mentioned earlier in this book.

Also in the 1980s, the Swedish researcher Hans-Arne Hansson at Gothenburg University recorded brain injuries in a group of radar operators, who had repaired military radar plant. They had become afflicted by such severe problems that they were unable to work. They were suffering memory losses and had difficulties in concentrating. Two of them had been afflicted with partial blindness. This study caused considerable interest in the USA where it was noted that the changes Hansson reported on could be directly linked to microwaves.

Henri Lai, at Washington University in Seattle, currently one of the most notable researchers when it comes to the biological effects of microwaves, has showed that there are co-effects of microwaves and various medicines. In a recently compiled summary of the state of research he mentions that the joint action of radio frequency radiation and chemicals can have a major effect on health.

Professor Henry Kues of the John Hopkins Applied Physics Laboratory in the USA reported something interesting at a research conference in Bologna, Italy, organized by the Bio-Electromagnetic Society in 1997. He said that in tests with medical students it had been found that relatively low levels of radio frequency waves can give significant effects both on the cornea and the retina. In a study, published in 1992, it had been found that endothelium cells in corneas had been destroyed when using a combination of microwaves and medicine used to treat glaucoma.

"I can't interpret it in any other way than that the specialist who has expressed his opinion in the case of Anders Lindström has gone outside his field of competence when he says that microwave radiation cannot cause the type of injury that Anders has," says Ragnar Forshufvud.

> Nowadays, when you measure the exposure of body parts to microwaves from a nearby source, the measurements are made on a simulation of the body part in question, usually the head. Results are not given as effect-densities but as Specific Absorption Rates (SAR), expressed in watts per kilogram.
>
> The World Health Organization's recommended limit is set at 2 watts per kilogram, but Henry Kues and his colleagues write that their data indicates that microwave pulses with a mean value of 0.26 watt per kilogram can have significant effects on

eyes that have been treated with eye medicines. The researchers chose to study the most common chemicals used to treat eyes. It is probable that other chemicals may be substantially more harmful to the eye.

The conclusion must be that there are no fixed limits for combinations of the type of chemicals and electromagnetic exposure that Anders Lindström has been subjected to.

But the expert on occupational and environmental medicine in Uppsala saw no risks when it came to chemicals either. In his report, he mentions that small tubes of epoxy adhesive were present on all workbenches and that this was "mixed drop by drop on a plate directly beside the work station." But he adds: "... small volumes, low concentrations."

Anders Lindström may also have been exposed to epoxy from heated circuit cards, something that the expert in Uppsala seems to be totally unaware of. If Anders became sensitized to the decomposition substances of epoxy, which reacted in combination with light, it is not so difficult to understand why he couldn't tolerate the environment he worked in. One only needs to make a comparison with the Svenska Fläkt employees, described in Chapter 3. The workers there had the most severe symptoms when all the machines were running and the strip lighting in the ceiling was switched on. Anders Lindström's work situation was even worse as he worked with microwaves.

Another quotation from the expert in Uppsala is: "Soldering, without use of efficiently functioning extractors, flux compounds. Exposure to solvents in the form of industrial spirits used for cleaning printed circuit cards, small volumes." Anders Lindström is very surprised: "There wasn't any kind of device to extract air from the testing areas, how can he write 'without efficiently functioning extractors'?" The gist of the letter from the expert is that nothing harmful had been present at Anders Lindström's place of work:

This type of complaint is often referred to as idiopathic, that is the causes are not known. Both of these conditions have been described a long time ago, before we became exposed to electromagnetic fields, microwaves, and other things around us nowadays. With respect to your other problems, chest and head pressure, twitchings in your legs, facial pain, and swelling, no one has been able to find an explanation. Nasal congestion and eye irritation (not the injury that was operated on!) can possibly have been caused by exposure to soldering fumes.

The specialist concludes the letter by saying that Anders Lindström's problems cannot depend on his work, "I can find no support for such a suspicion in scientific literature". "But I became sick at work," sighs Anders, despondently. "In the early stages I felt much better at weekends. When I had taken a holiday I was almost free from problems. At work I got sick again, unfortunately chronically ill in the end."

In January 1993 the Swedish Radiation Protection Institute, SSI, measured leakage fields in the same kind of workplace as the one in which Anders Lindström had worked. The documentation indicates that at a frequency of 869 megahertz, with the cover removed for trimming at two different power levels, 148 and 180 watts, at a distance of 0.1 meter from the final amplifier, the measurement obtained was 55 volts per meter. The set limit is 60 volts per meter.

Anders Lindström did not see this document until late spring 2001. It appears that Ericsson Radio System, in connection with Anders Lindström's case, had sent a totally different document to the regional social insurance office. The wrong document contained measurements on the sender itself, not the amplifier stages. Thanks to his stubbornness and decisiveness, Anders Lindström has finally got hold of the appropriate document.

The workplace at which the measurements were taken is similar to my old one. They did not take measurements for the final amplifier of the GSM 900 transmitter at my test station, but these are at least equivalent, he says.

The field strength, 55 volts per meter, is valid for a functional final amplifier. If the amplifier is faulty it can produce a greater field strength, exceeding the set limit. This may have happened often, as it was my job to find faults and repair them. My test station may have been a real hazard.

Anders Lindström points out that the SSI document has notes that a special cover ought to be used when trimming the final amplifier, because of the high field strength. Ericsson Radio System had neglected this. "This type of protective cover has been used at Ericsson at other test sites in Gävle, but none was used at the main factory's testing sites for the final amplifier in GSM transmitters," says Anders. He also found out that the field strength measured ought not to exceed one fifth of the set limit. In his case this would have meant 12 volts per meter.

It wasn't until 2000 that Anders Lindström got to know that he should have been able to have legal help via his union, the Swedish Metal Workers' Union, to get his occupational injury claim accepted. No one had told him earlier. Now something remarkable started to happen. Time and again an ombudsman at the union's local office in Gävle explained to Anders that it was too early to bring a lawyer to handle his occupational injury claim. The lowest authority, the regional social insurance office, must first reach a decision on whether it was a case of occupational injury or not. If the decision went against him, Anders had the right to appeal to two higher authorities and, if the claim was disallowed at both these courts, the ombudsman himself promised to help Anders to appeal to the highest authority.

I wouldn't have believed this if I hadn't spoken to this ombudsman several times. It is clear to anyone who understands a little of the Swedish occupational injuries laws that this was grave misinformation, aimed at misleading Anders Lindström. Few workers manage to handle their own cases at the three lowest authorities by themselves. This is exactly why the Swedish trade unions have formed a joint central organization, LO/TCO Legal Protection AB, to help members.

Local trade union bodies usually apply to the central organizations to cover costs. Something that most people know is that it is extremely difficult to acquire the right to appeal to the highest authority. For this to happen there have to be substantial new facts in the case. It could hardly be expected that Anders Lindström, whose sight is seriously impaired and who is unfamiliar with the legislation, would be able to handle all this by himself.

Over the phone the ombudsman in Gävle once told me that he was convinced that Anders Lindström had been injured at work but "you know we have powerful interests against us". It was clear that he was terrified at the thought of carrying out his duty to fight Ericsson Radio Systems. Anders Lindström was a lightweight compared to the giant that had promised to turn Gävle into a "global center for cell phone networks," as they put it. The company is the largest mobile telephony production unit in the Ericsson Group. In recent years production has become increasingly automated. Anders Lindström was just a fly in the ointment, an unpleasant reminder that employees' health was the price of progress when manual production was still in use.

The intention was that Anders Lindström should have a cornea transplant in his left eye in April 2001, but in consultation with his eye specialist, he has decided to wait. The rejection reactions following the operation on his right eye and his continued greatly reduced vision have deterred him. It is not a normal reaction after operations of this nature. He is not convinced that it is keratoconus he is suffering from. This is often a hereditary complaint. Nor can the doctors give a definite diagnosis. "I believe most things point to an eye injury that occurred at work, so I don't want to risk a second operation."

In 2003 the company doctor admitted that Anders Lindström's cornea had been affected by the soldering fumes he had worked in, in other words that it was a question of occupational illness.

In July 2003 the Metal Workers' Union in Stockholm promised that Anders Lindström would be given a lawyer. After almost six years, the fight for compensation could begin.

But in December 2003 nothing had happened. The union lawyer seemed not to understand the nature of the problems in the work place and Ericsson Radio System threatened to fire Anders Lindström because he had been on sick leave for so many years. The local union representatives said nothing in the meeting where the company offered a young man who had lost his sight compensation corresponding to little more than a month's salary.

13

Cover-up I:
Unwanted knowledge

If electro-hypersensitivity was suddenly to become an officially accepted diagnosis it would be interesting to ask the question how much of the Swedish research in this field would survive re-evaluation.

Many research reports, theses, and so-called consensus documents would be seen as irrelevant and hopelessly out of date, which is already true for a large number of them. The work being carried out by Associate Professor Olle Johansson at the Experimental Dermatology Unit, Karolinska Institute in Stockholm, belongs to that which I think would continue to be relevant. I am not alone in this opinion. Bo Walhjalt, a scientific theorist at the University of Gothenburg, has kept track of developments with respect to research into electro-hypersensitivity. Olle Johansson is, in Walhjalt's opinion, the only researcher who has consistently raised fundamental questions in this field:

> One could say that there's a smorgasbord of relevant questions that could be used to provide enlightenment. Olle Johansson has helped himself, but most other researchers avoid these matters as if they were a plague. Those who do touch on the field manipulate the questions so that nothing unpleasant is uncovered, knowing that it would not be good for their careers.

So, whilst Olle Johansson is driven by curiosity and the wish to discover what isn't known, mainstream researchers are cautious, covering up in case of unpleasant surprises.

Using advanced technology, Olle Johansson has shown that there are differences between normal skin in control groups and that of people suffering from VDU sickness. He has also extended our knowledge about skin in general. His discoveries have been sensational in several cases. It is no less sensational that his findings, though published in international scientific journals, are not included in Swedish summaries of the state of current research in the field.

In order to fully understand this official view it is necessary to look back over the past years. It all began in 1985 when the histopathologist and dermatologist Björn Lagerholm at the Dermatology Clinic at Karolinska Hospital raised the alarm about unusual changes in the skin of VDU-operators. The story is told in the first chapter of this book. The atmosphere in the Dermatology Clinic had become tense. Professor Sture Lidén and his younger colleague, Dr Mats Berg, succeeded, however, in the years that followed to get the message out that there wasn't anything to be alarmed about: VDUs were safe. There weren't any skin changes. Effectively, Björn Lagerholm's findings were clothed in silence.

Then, Olle Johansson popped up. He worked just across the road, heading the Experimental Dermatology Unit at the Karolinska Institute. It would prove to be impossible to smother his findings. He was still a young man who had progressed rapidly in his career and was already much sought after to give lectures abroad. He had taken his doctor's degree at the Faculty of Medicine, Karolinska Institute, his thesis being on neuropeptides in the central and peripheral nervous systems. Peptides are substances that carry messages between cells. In 1986 he became Associate Professor in Neurobiology, and in 1991 Associate Professor in Neuroscience. By chance he heard about people who had become sick and developed symptoms that they experienced as hypersensitivity to electromagnetic fields whilst working with VDUs. He was surprised that they were not taken seriously; as a neurobiologist, he thought that it was wrong to wave aside such symptoms as smarting and burning pains in the skin as "non-specific" and uninteresting. Using skin samples from people who had complaints after using VDUs, he made some interesting observations in a pilot study, encouraging him to pursue the matter further.

This decision had a major effect on his own fate. He became a "troublesome" researcher. Suddenly he noticed that it had begun to become difficult to find funding for his research. Since then he has been subjected to imputations and slanderous campaigns. But he also became something else – a researcher who climbed down from his ivory tower, making contact with a reality in which people could be deprived of their sickness allowances when they said that VDUs had caused their illness.

In the USA, it has been noticed for many years that researchers who bring to light inconvenient facts relating to electromagnetic radiation are frozen out and find it hard to get funding. Professor Henry Lai at Washington University in Seattle is one of the most recent cases in point. He is a respected researcher in the field. But, a few years ago when he observed that microwaves of the same kind as those used in GSM mobile phones could cause both single- and double-strand disruptions in the DNA of brain cells in rats, he abruptly found that he was no longer funded. He couldn't continue his research. Henry Lai took part in a conference in Sweden in autumn 1999. Suddenly he was handed a check from Mohammed al Fayed, one of the world's richest men, owner of the London department store, Harrods. Olle Johansson, in Sweden, seems to need a generous patron, too.

Nowadays, when it is often difficult to draw the boundary between university research and business activities, Olle Johansson is a very controversial person in Sweden. He was first to warn publicly that the extension of mobile telephony means that we are all subjects in a gigantic biological experiment. He also told the general public at an early stage that what is known as the SAR value, referred to by the authorities, is only valid when heating takes place and that biological effects exist at much lower levels. Thus, perhaps it isn't unexpected that it has become difficult for him to receive public funding.

The observations Björn Lagerholm had made, that VDU operators with different symptoms had raised levels of mast cells, interested Olle Johansson. Mast cells react, for example, in asthma and allergies. Symptoms such as itching, pricking, and smarting pain arise when mast cells release histamine and heparin. UV light and certain x-rays can cause mast cells to secrete these substances.

In 1992 and 1994 Johansson produced method studies concerning staining techniques for this type of cell. Soon afterwards he presented a sensational study, proving that histamine can be found even in nerve fibers in the skin. "This, of course, overthrows many of the models used to explain itching, smarting pain, swellings, etc," he commented. Later, he and his colleague, Peng-Yue Liu, conducted a control study in which 15 healthy volunteers were compared with an equal number of electro-hypersensitive subjects. The latter were shown to have considerably more mast cells. These were also larger and more superficial in the dermis, the deeper inner layer of skin, than was the case in the control group.

Olle Johansson and his colleagues also developed a method to study mast cells and their relationship to nerve fibers that contained peptides simultaneously in skin and mucous membranes. One of the questions that Olle Johansson asked himself was: What happens to mast cells in the skin of healthy volunteers when they are placed in front of VDUs or TVs, two devices with the same cathode ray tube construction? This was a natural question because he had observed distinct changes in similar provocation tests on VDU patients. So, he carried out an open provocation test in which he examined skin biopsies from 13 volunteers prior to, and after, 2 and 4 hours of exposure to TVs and VDUs. None of them had suffered from skin complaints earlier, nor any known allergies and they were all non-smokers. None of them reported any subjective reactions during the provocation test. No objective symptoms were seen in any of them during, or after, the test. The number of mast cells in the dermis of 5 of the 13 volunteers had, however, increased after the provocation test. The cells had moved closer to the surface in nine of the volunteers, and also changed in different respects. The number of mast cells returned to the previous count 24 hours after the experiment.

What was sensational was that normal mast cells, in the skin of healthy people, can change in front of common TV sets and VDUs. Olle Johansson comments that it is difficult to explain this in any other way than it being an effect of electric or magnetic fields. Some chemical in the surrounding air may, possibly, have played a part in this connection but chemicals were not measured in the test. As none of the volunteers had felt any subjective reactions, it is nevertheless difficult to argue for a psychological model to explain matters, he points out.

In 2000, together with a colleague, Shabnam Gangi, he presented a theoretical model as to how mast cells and the substances secreted by them, for example histamine, heparin, and serotonin, could explain sensitivity to electric and/or magnetic fields. This was published in the journal *Medical Hypotheses*. Johansson and Gangi refer to studies, including their own, showing that electromagnetic radiation affects mast cells so that the tiny grains that contain histamine and other substances are broken down. Cellular changes also take place in what are known as dendritic cells. It is not known whether this effect occurs directly or indirectly.

When inflammatory substances such as histamine from the mast cells spread in the skin, redness and edemas arise, as well as itching and pain. Similarly the dendritic cells can secrete somatostatin, a peptide hormone, which, in turn, can give rise to a subjective feeling of inflammation and even light sensitivity. These are among the symptoms that VDU-injured people have reported. Johansson and Gangi point out that mast cells are also found in heart tissues. They refer to studies showing that electromagnetic fields affect heart functions and suggest that this effect may simply be due to electromagnetic fields first affecting mast cells in heart tissues, especially in the heart valves. The electromagnetic fields might initially affect mast cells, releasing histamine, which excites the dendritic cells. Alternatively the dendritic cells, alone or together with mast cells, might be directly affected by electromagnetic fields.

Olle Johansson has found considerable changes in dendritic cells that contain somatostatin in a series of studies on samples of skin from electro-hypersensitive patients. This type of cell is also found in joints and in the brain. Today there are more and more international studies on mast cells forthcoming. An Australian researcher, Peter French, has shown that the production of histamine is almost doubled following exposure to electromagnetic radiation in the form of microwaves similar to those that mobile phones emit. He has also shown that these frequencies hinder the effect of conventional anti-histamine medicines.

Björn Lagerholm and Olle Johansson were early in making very important observations. But their findings have never been regarded as interesting in Sweden, in the circles that deal with research into electro-hypersensitivity. It has never been fully clarified how the establishment, which consists of researchers and funding bodies, really set about striking skin research from the agenda in this context.

It has been said, "no one has been able to verify these findings". The truth is that Olle Johansson has been the only person to use advanced microscope technology to study biopsies from this group of patients. Routine histopathology has been used to examine VDU-injured people in a few cases, e.g. at the University Hospital in Umeå, where biopsies have been taken in certain cases. But the skin specialist there, Berndt Stenberg, has said that they didn't have access to the same advanced technology as Olle Johansson. Other than Olle Johansson, no one in Sweden has made skin biopsies for this category of patients for many years.

Neurological symptoms have been brought to the foreground in the debate, without clarification that skin is an integral part of the complex interplay in the body.

Professor Gun Agrup at the Clinic for Occupational Dermatology, University Hospital in Lund, got money through Ericsson at the beginning of the 1990s for a provocation study. Her study did not cover the electro-hypersensitive Ericsson employees, but dealt with an entirely different group of patients with similar problems. She chose to omit biopsy studies, which originally were to have been taken care of by Olle Johansson. "We're letting him continue with his own studies, should there be any findings, he may just as well present them himself," she said when I asked her why no biopsies were to be taken in her study.

On that occasion Olle Johansson had about US$ 1500 at his disposal for research. Ericsson had made it quite clear that he was not included in the circle of researchers that they would give funding to.

In a 1997 edition of the Danish-German journal *Experimental Dermatology* there was a very interesting article in which skin changes in VDU-operators was systematically compared with known injuries arising from exposure to UV light, x-rays and radioactivity. The authors were Olle Johansson and Shabnam Gangi. Whilst there isn't any extensive knowledge of the skin conditions of electro-hypersensitive people, there is ample international literature on injuries caused by UV light and radioactivity. Gangi and Johansson had made a systematic summary of available research and compared it with their own. They found similarities throughout with respect to how mast cells and dendritic cells, as for example Langerhans' cells, react to UV light, radioactivity and electromagnetic fields of the type they have exposed their volunteers to. This points towards Björn Lagerholm being right from the start when he claimed that VDU patients hade injuries "as if caused by radiation".

Gangi and Johansson conclude their comprehensive summary with a reflection that a major part of the electromagnetic radiation that we are exposed to nowadays is a result of developments over recent decades; the question is whether or not our skins have sufficient defense mechanisms to cope with the new situation.

Microwaves are now an important part of our surroundings. Olle Johansson was first in the world to conduct double-blind tests to find out if those who claim they are electro-hypersensitive could tell whether or not a mobile phone was switched on. Of seven people taking part in the test, one was right all the time. Two said that the phone was on when the box, in which the phone was thought to have been, was empty. Later it was found that there was a military source nearby that was emitting high-frequency radiation. This may have contributed to the symptoms experienced by those taking part in the tests.

Olle Johansson has constantly been accused of not sticking to the subject at hand. Each time he has applied for funding from RALF, the Council for Working Life Research, the Council has requested him to specially indicate which of his published works has "relevance in the matter of electro-hypersensitivity". The question itself is interesting; how can you determine what is relevant with respect to an illness that has no official diagnosis and is thought by many to be imagined?

As Olle Johansson's special field is the skin, its various cells, nerve fibers, and signal substances, it is quite natural that he concerns himself with reactions in the skin. He has even pointed to the necessity of studying healthy skin and mucous membranes, if deviations in the skin of electro-hypersensitive subjects are to be examined: "I have tried to find out what happens in normal skin in order to lay a foundation of neurological building blocks." But RALF's constant question has been: What mechanism can explain the skin changes you have found in the electro-hypersensitive group? To which Olle Johansson replies: "Shabnam Gangi and I have produced two papers in which we discuss possible mechanisms that may cause these symptoms. It seems that RALF has not noticed them."

When Olle Johansson has presented pioneer discoveries as to the general nature of human skin, it has been obvious that some of the observations have direct relevance in this connection. This is true, for example of the discovery of nerve fibers that are only 0.01–0.04 millimeters from the surface of the horny layer of the epidermis in areas of thin skin like that in the face. That these fibers are present could contribute to an explanation of the itching and pains that electro-hypersensitive people report. It may be assumed that the fibers send impulses including some to the autonomic nervous system, says Olle Johansson.

In the beginning of the Swedish VDU-debate, some professors explained that the nerves are so deeply embedded in humans that it is impossible for them to react to electromagnetic fields, radon daughters, etc. This can now be contradicted by Olle Johansson. Thousands of VDU-operators around the world have itching feelings and pain in their fingertips, wrists, and shoulders. This doesn't seem especially surprising even to an amateur if it is the case that nerve fibers in fingertips react to the electromagnetic fields from keyboards and mice and that these impulses can be transported on to wrists and shoulders. Olle Johansson has not shown this. It is my own reflection arising after many years of meeting young people with painful wrists and shoulders. I find it difficult to believe that it is only a question of RSI, repetitive strain injury, which the discussion has been about. Not when giving thought to the rapid "pain career" experienced nowadays by very young people. Whilst traveling to find material for an article, at one workplace I met two young women in their twenties who had been obliged to have their wrists operated on, a woman who had severe eye problems, a woman who started to have eczema on her arms whilst working at an illuminated layout table and several people with skin complaints in their faces. I am not saying that RSI doesn't play a part in the pain arising in joints and muscles, but there are also other factors that company doctors seldom consider.

Olle Johansson's discovery of the existence of nerve fibers 0.01–0.04 millimeters from the surface of the skin was covered in a 1990 edition of the journal *Cell and Tissue Research*. In 1999 the General Director of the Swedish Institute of Radiation Protection stated that he could not see that Olle Johansson had published anything connected to electro-hypersensitivity. The Institute had not renewed their studies of deposits of radon daughters on a doll in front of a VDU – studies that had been discontinued in 1986, after a few experiments. And yet they explained that radiation would not be able to affect under the skin's surface. They took no notice of Olle Johansson's findings.

Reports by Professor Denis L. Henshaw at Bristol University, UK, on how radon daughters and other air pollutants gather round electrical equipment, both in- and outdoors, have not been of interest to the Institute either. Nor do the British radiation protection authorities seem to care about Henshaw's highly interesting hypothesis that this could be the mechanism explaining the over-representation of cancer that has been found in connection with low-frequency electromagnetic fields. Olle Johansson would like to conduct studies starting with Henshaw's findings. For example, it would be possible to apply various chemical substances to the skin and study what happens in fields from VDUs, mobile phones, etc:

> Researchers with special knowledge of particle migration are needed for more sophisticated studies. I suspect that during migration in a rapidly alternating electromagnetic field, particles, which in the first instance appear to be harmless, may penetrate the skin as when being tattooed. Such an effect could be the devastating co-factor towards skin damage and electro-hypersensitivity. Each factor in isolation, radiation or chemicals, may be harmless but together they may cause injuries.

It appears to be the case that, if the term electro-hypersensitivity is not used, some experts are unable to realize that new observations may be relevant for the group in question. When Olle Johansson found that melanocytes, cells in the skin that form pigmentation, can be "factories" that produce serotonin, it did not lack relevance with respect to electro-hypersensitivity either.

Many doctors have experimented by prescribing anti-depression medicines, such as Anafranil, Cipramil, and Prozac, for patients in this category. Thanks to the discovery of the hitherto unknown role played by melanocytes, Olle Johansson realized that these medicines could have very negative effects in general, but especially for this group of patients, who are often hypersensitive to light. In the worst cases, the medicines could lead to a deterioration of the skin's protection against light and other radiation, and, thereby, to tumors of melanocytes, usually referred to as malignant melanoma.

The medicines mentioned above have the ability to affect the uptake by cells of serotonin, a substance that forms the hormone melatonin, of importance to our biorhythm. The nightmare scenario that Olle Johansson fears is that an increased amount of serotonin in the skin could lead to receptors for melatonin in the melanocytes beginning to react to serotonin. The result could be that the melanocytes are no longer able to produce sufficient amounts of melanin pigment. The skin's protective system would become a sieve, letting in light, and other radiation.

The background to prescribing these anti-depressive medicines to electro-hypersensitive patients was research results showing that the amount of melatonin can be affected by electromagnetic fields. No one realized that there could be risks involved. In addition to Olle Johansson's apprehensions there is also a risk of becoming dependent on the drugs. Some of the electro-hypersensitive people who have been treated with them have told me that they have walked about in a daze, like zombies.

✖

Olle Johansson's scientific articles do not contain any absolutely certain statements about the cause of the remarkable changes he has observed in the skin of electro-hypersensitive people. It may be a question of electromagnetic fields, or chemicals, or some other factor, is the way he usually expresses himself. In the spirit of scientific objectivity, he has always been particularly anxious to mention "techno-stress," the theory cherished by those who slander him, even if he has never really believed that this theory would provide anything useful.

> No, that's true, I believe less and less in psychological factors and note that this model for explanation doesn't have many supporters outside Sweden. On the other hand I'm becoming increasingly convinced that other factors such as radiation and chemicals are involved.
>
> The number of scientific publications that show effects from electromagnetic fields is rapidly growing. They cover cells and cell functions, tissue cultures, and animal trials. I'm also thinking about blind-coded, controlled experiments on people who have had raised blood pressure in radio frequency fields. How such results can be explained away as techno-stress beats me.
>
> It is not possible to explain, nor explain away, these results using psychological factors. It is a question of radiation or chemicals, or perhaps a combination. Above all, I think it is important to investigate synergistic effects.

But he is not especially impressed that measures have been started on what substances are emitted from the plastics used in the electronics industry. In his opinion, it's like trying to find a needle in a haystack. Researchers will be tied up in pointless search, perhaps for some decades to come. Manufacturers have the answers, but external researchers are forced to conduct their studies by trial and error.

I think the state should simply force manufacturers to produce a list of all the substances they have mixed together when producing these plastics. When we have the list we can test the substances directly on skin, looking for hypersensitivity reactions and cell changes that are clinically verifiable.

If representatives of the manufacturing industry claim that the substances are harmless, I suggest we carry out tests using them as subjects. Otherwise, for ethical reasons, we have to stick to animal testing, for example on pig's skin. I suspect that, in reality, the substances in question are extremely harmful.

Some of the chemicals present in electronic devices are capable of acting as acetylcholinesterase inhibitors. This is an enzyme that breaks down acetylcholine, a signal substance found both in the central and the autonomic nervous systems. This balance is delicate and can be affected by a number of chemical substances as well as by electromagnetic radiation. This, in turn, leads to effects on breathing, heart, blood vessels, etc.

Acetylcholinesterase inhibitors can lead to an increase in activities in the autonomic nervous system, for example in the form of altered sensitivity to light, flickering, etc. This increased irritability can very well be thought of as leading to general, chronic fatigue of the type many people report. So, I ask: An imbalance in the autonomic nervous system has been observed in electro-hypersensitive persons. Is there something that can explain this hypersensitivity, which, in most cases has arisen in connection with operating VDUs? "Yes," Olle Johansson answers. "If the layers of cells closest to the surface of the skin become damaged it is quite natural to assume that there will be effects on the autonomic nervous system." Perhaps it should be added that organic phosphates, of the type found in VDUs, can create this imbalance in the autonomic nervous system, by hindering the activity of acetylcholinesterase enzymes. Do the effects of chemicals have similarities to those you see at the microscopic level when examining skin that has been exposed to electromagnetic fields? Olle Johansson answers:

> That's an interesting question, but as far as I know, what effects chemicals in electronics may have, has not been studied. From what you can read in common consumer information, you may come to the conclusion that there are clear parallels between our observations concerning skin and some of the injuries that these chemicals can cause.
>
> I suspect that certain substances may have effects on lymphocytes, Langerhans' cells and mast cells. Common histopathological studies are lacking to a great extent, and more advanced methods, like those we use in our studies of skin, have only been used sporadically.

In 1995 RALF, the Council for Working Life Research, asked five foreign doctors to evaluate the competence of the research teams that were funded by the Council to conduct studies in the field of skin. This evaluation was published in one of RALF's regular series of publications.

The five foreign doctors' assessment of the work done by Olle Johansson and his colleagues was full of superlatives. They had done top-class scientific work. The discovery of intra-epidermal nerve fibers in normal skin was mentioned: "... the findings open new perspectives for study and understanding of skin inflammation and how itching arises. The method used to demonstrate nerves that contain histamine and the whole area of histamine-immunohistochemistry is elegant and of great scientific value." The mast cells and other findings in electro-hypersensitive persons were also noted as being "interesting and new". "A competent and highly productive team of researchers," the foreign doctors wrote.

But it was obvious that there had been discussions behind the scenes that the foreign experts had taken notice of. When it came to voicing an opinion on Olle Johansson's need for funding for fur-ther research into electro-hypersensitivity they suddenly express themselves in exactly the same wording as that used by those in Sweden who oppose the question in general, and Olle Johansson in particular. They stated that the group of electro-hypersensitive people was "extremely heterogeneous" and impossible to conduct systematic studies on. They concluded by saying "further funding for the projects proposed concerning skin problems from VDUS cannot be recommended at present". It is hard to believe that it is the same group of experts who wrote both the evaluation and the recommendation.

The chairman of the group that so categorically speaks against funding for the sole Swedish researcher who was examining the skin of those with VDU-related injuries was Matti Hannuksela, senior physician at the Southern Karelian Hospital in Lappeenranta, Finland. In a telephone interview I made with him he found it difficult to recall Olle Johansson: "Was he the one who was investigating magnetic fields?" he asked, finally. When he recalled who Olle Johansson was, he went on: "As you know, there were five experts and we were all convinced that his investigations were not of high class." But," I responded, in fact, you wrote that his research was of very high class? "Did we?"

Olle Johansson told me that he happened to discuss electro-magnetic fields with the foreign doctors during a lunch. They didn't seem to know much about the subject, so he had tried to explain a few basic concepts, but they had not seemed to understand at all. One of the doctors had expressed surprise that the question of electro-hypersensitivity was taken seriously in Sweden. His firm view was that patients who think they react to electromagnetic fields "must be mad". The foreign doctors had been selected on the basis of their knowledge of dermatological research. They can't be blamed for not being experts in electromagnetic fields. But why were they ever asked to express an opinion on something that they either didn't know about or were prejudiced towards? After this, RALF was able to refer to international expertise when they continued to put the dampers on Olle Johansson's research.

✖

Olle Johansson has often been pessimistic about his possibilities of conducting the research he wants to. It isn't just a matter of funding, it also concerns the space required for patients to be tested, etc. Over a number of years he has successively had less space at his disposal.

I asked Lars Olson, Head of the Department for Neuroscience at the Karolinska Institute, how the Institute actually views research into electro-hypersensitivity. "I have the greatest respect for Olle Johansson's research. It is important and will, of course, continue," he answered. But Lars Olson made no substantial effort to keep open the practical possibility of Olle Johansson's continuing the research in question. On the contrary, he contributed towards curtailing resources, if not actually obliterating them. "I see no future for this research without substantial public sector financed support. The Swedish community is not going to provide support," was Olle Johansson's own comment.

He has spoken publicly in interviews with the mass media in an increasingly frank manner on the full-scale experiments being carried out on the entire population in the western World, which the development of mobile telephony entails. He has become a thorn in the side of the authorities and, of course, industry.

A former head, as well as an assistant head of the department, at the Karolinska Institute once tried to silence him by demanding that all his public statements on health hazards and electromagnetic radiation must be subject to prior approval. They soon realized that this would be an illegal act. They were forced to back down. Behind their concern lay thoughts about the danger of withdrawal of financial support to the Karolinska Institute from the private sector. Demands for control and censoring have once again been raised in various debate articles during recent years, written by a number of professors, some of whom are deeply involved in the commercial re-structuring of the Karolinska Institute.

There are, however, other ways of punishing those who do not toe to the line. Recently Olle Johansson found that he could not be promoted to Professor of Neuroscience, despite his having 455 publications to his name. The reason was that his research concerning electro-hypersensitivity was seen to be "dissipated" and to lack "a completely clear line". His earlier research in other fields had, however, been praised and his teaching skills were regarded as being ample to warrant his promotion to professor. The grounds on which his studies concerning electro-hypersensitivity were said to "lack a completely clear line" were not clarified. How "a clear line" should look in this matter would be very interesting to know.

The words of Bo Walhjalt, the scientific theorist, have come true. In an interview that I had with him a couple of years ago he forecast what would happen: Olle Johansson would be made to pay for his frankness. Bo Walhjalt quoted the French philosopher, Michael Foucault, who spoke of "the enclosed" and "the excluded" in the academic world.

> That which is excluded is not spoken of – it is taboo. So that no one steps over the boundary, there are guardians who, via lobbying or mobbing, disarm those who are guilty of the unacceptable. At the same time this means that the free furtherance of knowledge, the prime task of researchers, is hindered.

When Olle Johansson was once again refused research funding, protests came from associations for electro-hypersensitive people in both Sweden and Finland at the end of 2001 and early in 2002. Despite recommendations from some of the foremost researchers in Sweden, the authorities were indifferent towards his application, which concerned studying mast cells in the skin, lymphocytes, and melanocytes in relation to VDU-injuries and electro-hypersensitivity.

One of those who supported the application was Lars Römnbäck, Professor in Neurology at Gothenburg University. He wrote that the proposed research project could contribute knowledge about the reaction of skin cells to electromagnetic fields as well as about signaling mechanisms between the skin and nerve systems. In 2002 the funding authority referred formally to a lack of means. When the same authority rejected the same application in 2003 they stated that the application "had not been able to compete with other applications". In that year Olle Johansson's application was the only one specifically concerned with the complex of problems related to electro-hypersensitivity.

14

Cover-up II:
Consensus at any price

The Fifth General Directorate of the European Commission had for many years received numerous enquiries about electro-hyper-sensitivity. When some of the civil servants at the Directorate met the Swede Ulf Bergqvist, the idea was put forward that someone ought to produce a summary of what was available in this field. Ulf Bergqvist jumped at the idea and made a formal application for funding. It resulted in the publication *Possible Health Implications of Subjective Symptoms and Electromagnetic Fields*, published by the Directorate in 1997 for use in Europe.

Several people contributed to the publication, but Ulf Bergqvist is one of two editors and the person who reports about the situation in Sweden. He was a senior lecturer at Linköping University College of Technology, but had also worked as a research engineer at the National Institute for Working Life in Stockholm.

When, in autumn 1985, Björn Lagerholm, the skin specialist and histopathologist at Karolinska Hospital in Stockholm raised the alarm that he had observed strange changes when using light microscopy to examine skin from people with VDU-related complaints, it was Ulf Bergqvist who quickly informed the media that computer screens could not be the cause.

Björn Lagerholm commented that he had reported what he had seen under the microscope, but was not going to get involved in technical aspects, they were not his field. Then he withdrew from the stage. Ulf Bergqvist was to remain on stage as a keen debater until he passed away in autumn 2001. His doctoral thesis was an epidemiological study of eye complaints and other common problems connected to using computers in some office environments. His studies had nothing to do with electro-hypersensitive people, he declared. But on this particular question he was to become an expert, often consulted by Swedish authorities. He was influential also outside Sweden through the UN bodies WHO (World Health Organisation) and ILO (International Labor Organisation).

In the EU publication that he edited he hardly does justice to the Swedish situation. The selection of research reports is very limited. There is no picture of the real situation in Sweden, with big companies electrosanitizing the work environments, for example. Björn Lagerholm, whose findings started the Swedish debate, is named in a footnote. Information about Olle Johansson's research at the Karolinska Institute is so meager that hardly anyone who isn't already familiar with it can grasp what it is all about.

When I interviewed Ulf Bergqvist and asked about the reason for this, he said that he had not been aware of Björn Lagerholm's findings of abnormal amounts of mast cells in the skin of VDU patients. And even if he had heard about it he couldn't give consideration to "rumors and such like," he explained to me. He only quoted research reports, a narrow selection at that. Björn Lagerholm had not produced any research report on these findings, having only written an article in *Läkartidningen*, a Swedish medical journal. This is how very important observations, made by a skillful histopathologist, and research reports, published in scientific journals by a neurobiologist, were hidden from the readers of the publication Ulf Bergqvist edited. Readers in EU countries were expected to be content with Bergqvist's selection.

The main theme in the booklet was that one ought to take a united stance towards these subjective symptoms in order to calm the general public. There was nothing to worry about.

Journalists were identified as an important target group to be used towards achieving consensus. Consensus was the key word also in a report on electro-hypersensitivity, presented to the Swedish Government in December 2000 by three experts. Ulf Bergqvist was one of them. They were called "the RALF experts," because the Government had commissioned the report from RALF, the Swedish Council for Working Life Research. Their task was to provide an account of Swedish and international research findings within the field of electro-hypersensitivity and the possible health risks from electromagnetic radiation as a whole.

Seldom has a more controversial document seen the light of day than the final report that these three experts handed over to the Government. But the report could be seen as tailor-made for a government that wanted to hasten technological developments without having to consider people who had become sick in front of VDUs and those who now said they become sick because of microwaves from mobile phones. The Ministry of Industry, Employment, and Communications, which received it, couldn't have wished for a more welcome message than the conclusion in the report.

The most important message seemed to be that people in general did not think that there was something to worry about but that there were "certain smaller groups," firmly convinced that electromagnetic fields do constitute health risks. According to the RALF group this conviction in itself was a health risk, which needed to be "dealt with" in some way.

The RALF report was strongly skewed towards mobile phones. VDUs were dismissed as being almost a non-current issue. With respect to electro-hypersensitivity the experts state that the results of scientific studies oppose the idea that electric and magnetic fields could be a sufficient, or necessary, factor to cause symptoms in those who claim they are electro-hypersensitive. The politicians were lulled into a sense of security, believing that the researchers had done everything in their power to fully investigate the matter. The RALF experts stated that interest now was being directed towards other factors as "individual qualities such as imbalance in the autonomic nervous system". No mention was made of the doubts expressed by many people about whether the provocation studies conducted in Sweden were the correct method for examining this group of patients. It had often been the case that people who took part in them were exposed in laboratories to what might be called pure electromagnetic fields, without regard being taken to the fact that "pure" electricity doesn't occur any longer in our usual surroundings as the network is contaminated by disturbances. Not to mention that there have not yet been provocation studies with control over the whole spectrum of electromagnetic radiation, including UV, let alone chemical aspects. In very few technical studies has interest been concentrated on the equipment people have used and in these studies test people have never been involved. .

The question about the possible role of chemicals in this context had been raised very forcefully by several speakers in a public hearing RALF had arranged on 8 March 2000 in Stockholm. One of those to speak on that occasion was Yvonne Thunell, BSc. (Econ), who had taken great interest in the research into electro-hypersensitivity for many years, finding it insufficient and fragmented. She asked for an overall strategy on the part of the authorities and experts responsible for research in this field and "an ambition to find the causes". Above all she highlighted the combination effects:

> Chemicals and radiation are two factors that have had an explosive development in our environment. All kinds of chemicals as well as what we call electro-smog, in the form of radio-waves, microwaves, and also more low frequency fields in our homes and at work have increased. Research, however, is way behind the increased exposure. It is important to know that there is no research into the biological effects of the combination of chemicals and radiation. It is not known what happens when a person with a high load of chemicals is exposed

to electromagnetic fields. Nor are there methods available to measure these chemicals.

She had followed the fate of a boy falling ill at the age of nine in connection with renovation at his school and an installation of powerful fluorescent tubes. Like many other children he had grown up in surroundings with numerous electronic devices in which brominated flame-retardants and other chemicals were present. When blood samples from the boy were analyzed at Stockholm University, very high levels of several substances, including brominated flame-retardants, were found. He immediately began to get better after the fluorescent tubes in the school had been taken out and his home had been electro-sanitized. Yvonne Thunell had noted that certain chemicals such as solvents, adhesives, exhaust gases, and, above all, chemicals from electronics, started the boy's symptoms.

Another speaker at the RALF hearing, Helen Bertilson, trained both as a nurse and a researcher, spoke along similar lines and asked for interdisciplinary research. An unbiased survey of the circumstances surrounding those who had fallen ill and hypersensitive might reveal surprising links between things like chemicals from new computer equipments, emissions in damp buildings and perhaps amalgam or other mixtures of metals and materials in teeth, she said.

Perhaps what is most remarkable about how the RALF group acted was that they inquired into the symptoms suffered by electro-hypersensitive people only to ignore them. "Write and tell us about your symptoms – we will publish your letters," they wrote in newspaper announcements. They received 415 replies, written by some of the best-educated people in Sweden ever to have occupational injuries. Many of those who replied held university degrees; people who had used computers as their most cherished tools, but had seen their careers go up in smoke when their hypersensitivity broke out. In addition, 33 verbal contributions were given at the aforementioned hearing by some of the afflicted and other very knowledgeable people. These, too, had expected that their input would be printed and passed on to the Swedish Government.

What happened to the 415 letters and the contributions to the debate at the hearing? Gunnel Färm, the Director General of RALF, said there was no money available to publish them. In December 2000, when the final report from the experts was finished, a box full of the letters and speeches was sent over to the Ministry of Industry, Employment, and Communications. A box filled with letters – who had time to look into them? Perhaps it was assumed that they would be forgotten after a while. In their final report the RALF experts had written that the letters were "of very varied content" and that it was not possible to use them to come to any conclusions about the symptoms and complaints arising in connection with electro-hypersensitivity. The letters might have remained in the box at the Ministry, but this was not their fate. Rigmor Granlund-Lind and John Lind, two college teachers, requested copies of the letters, sat down and read them. They found them be a goldmine of knowledge, with shocking descriptions that pulled the carpet from under the official report to the Government. Rigmor Granlund-Lind and John Lind have written a book about the letters. The title of the book, published in Swedish in 2003, is *Svart på vitt* (*Black on white*). I have heard several researchers spontaneously express the view that the book is full of concrete lines of approach for research.

Never before in Swedish history has such a large group of people with occupational injuries given so well put and concise accounts of how they have fallen ill, what has triggered their symptoms, and what they think about different explanations. The letters also reveal how authorities and most experts have ignored the knowledge and experience of those afflicted, year after year.

Using the letters as a basis Professor Emeritus Jan Rennerfelt, a chemist with biotechnology and ecology as specialties, compiled diagrams of the symptoms of those afflicted. These show which factors have triggered and maintained the symptoms of the letter writers. They also show which the most common symptoms are. The diagrams present a picture that in no way agrees with the one presented to the Government by the RALF experts.

Hypersensitivity to light is almost entirely overlooked in the RALF report. The letters, on the other hand, show that hypersensitivity to light is the second most common symptom after skin complaints such as itching and burning sensations. Perhaps it's possible that those who wrote the letters would have placed this hypersensitivity at the top of the list if they had been aware what effects light can have in connection with certain chemicals.

Following skin symptoms and hypersensitivity to light comes eye complaints, fatigue and weakness, heart problems and high blood pressure, respiratory and lung complaints, aching joints and muscles, loss of memory, dizziness, concentration difficulties, numbness, hearing problems including tinnitus, and sleeping problems. Shivering and cramp were mentioned in no fewer than 22 letters. Even speech problems were reported in a few cases.

The letters showed that computer work was the clearly dominant factor in causing the symptoms. Chemicals and copying machines were mentioned, but not that many. As Jan Rennerfelt points out it could be the case that chemicals emitted from computer equipment were a decisive factor in causing illness without the persons concerned themselves making this special distinction.

For those who already were hypersensitive, computers were once again noted as making symptoms worse, followed by other electrical installations, mobile phones, lighting, radio/TV, cars, chemicals, and dental care. Amalgam fillings in teeth were mentioned as a very important triggering factor.

The RALF experts had, in their report to the Swedish Government, toned down VDU-problems and indicated that the focus had shifted to mobile phones. This is in direct contrast to the first-hand reports in the letters from those afflicted.

✖

Consensus was the goal for the RALF experts. Their idea was that one ought to come to some kind of consensus as to what electro-hypersensitivity is. A lot of effort was put into series of conferences aimed at reaching general agreement: Does this sickness exist at all, and if so, how should it be described? This was rather remarkable insofar as the Government had not requested that consensus be reached. But Ulf Bergqvist and also Dr. Lena Hillert, another of the RALF experts, were already known to want consensus in this area. Over the years both had maintained that there was no cause for concern about health risks from VDUs, mobile phones, or other sources of electromagnetic radiation. In various contexts they had impatiently sought consensus on electro-hypersensitivity. Throughout the entire process of the governmental commission Bergqvist and Hillert were also members of Telia Mobile's scientific advisory council. It's not usual practice in Sweden for experts called upon by the Government to work for industry in the same area at the same time. Telia is the national telephone company in Sweden.

Ulf Bergqvist had even more reason to avoid have dealings with the telecom industry; he was also a member of the International Commission on Non-Ionizing Radiation Protection, ICNIRP, a committee whose tasks included producing European recommendations for maximum permissible values with respect to microwave radiation from mobile phones. ICNIRP members are expected to be completely independent of all commercial interest.

RALF ceased to exist at year-end 2000 in connection with a total reorganization of research authorities. Criticism of the way the governmental commission was handled thereby lost media interest. Who cares what happened in an authority that no longer exists? But the RALF report is today used everywhere in the Swedish society – and surely also abroad – as an argument against the electro-hypersensitive people.

15

Cover-up III: Components of a "sickness bomb"

"Disarm the sickness bomb!" was the heading of a debate article in a minor Swedish daily newspaper, published in July 2001, and signed by several experts and politicians. The message went on: "More and more people have become ill because of the air we breathe, the food we eat, the water we drink, the machines we use to work with, and the housing we live in."

In one short, sharp sentence, the writers summarize important factors behind the new hypersensitivity syndromes, fast becoming one of the greatest problems of western societies. They echo worldwide concern with widespread physical reactions to the many different forms of pollution of our planet. Without going into concrete factors, they raise the remarkable fact that so few people make a direct link between the increasingly frequent alarms about dangerous chemicals and other environmental risks and new illnesses. Words like environmental influences and environmentally conditioned illnesses are seldom used in connection with those who become ill. Admittedly there are discussions on sick building syndrome, multiple chemical sensitivity, fibromyalgia, electro-hypersensitivity, chronic fatigue and immune dysfunction syndrome and the other illnesses, which are sometimes summarized under the heading neurosomatic illnesses, but experts and authorities like to regard them as separate phenomena, considerable resources being committed to investigate their link to the psyche.

It was one of the writers of the article, Professor Emeritus Robert Olin, who introduced the term neurosomatic illnesses. During his active years he worked as a clinician and scientist, dealing with issues within preventive, occupational, and internal medicine and epidemiology. For the last years he has focused on finding explanations to long-term pain and fatigue. In his opinion, that which is affected above all in these groups of people is the central nervous system, immune defense, and hormonal, endocrine, systems.

The view held by the writers of the article is that the hundreds of thousands afflicted in Sweden alone have been made invisible. They are too ill to make themselves heard and medical research about them is almost non-existent. It will be a long time before the insignificant research findings that have been obtained can be used clinically. Doctors, who don't know how to help this category of patients, often choose to label their sickness as imaginary. They give them psychiatric diagnoses and prescribe psychopharmaceutical preparations, treatment which, according to the authors of the article, only makes their medical condition worse, as many of them are hypersensitive to chemicals. Those who are sick are hidden away in many ways. Those suffering from fibromyalgia are often members of associations against rheumatism, even though most experts agree that their condition is not really a rheumatic one. Thus, it becomes difficult to find accurate information about them.

Another of those who took the initiative to write the article was a journalist, Gertie Gladnikoff. She is chairman of a regional organization in northern Sweden for those suffering from chronic fatigue. The name given to this syndrome in Sweden is myalgic encephalomyelitis (me), referring to an inflammation of the brain and spinal cord. Agreement has, however, not been reached on the use of this term. The most common international term used is chronic fatigue syndrome, coined by the American health authorities. A more accurate term, used by those who suffer from the illness, is chronic fatigue and immune dysfunction syndrome, CFIDS.

When I phoned Gertie Gladnikoff she told me that in this northern part of Sweden a network has been set up between various groups suffering from environmentally conditioned illnesses such as electro-hypersensitivity and chemical hypersensitivity. Moreover, many of the members of the ME association regard themselves as being sensitive to electromagnetic fields. The same is true for many of those who are hypersensitive to chemicals. Thus, the symptoms of the groups overlap.

"Neurosomatically ill" is what the members of the network, inspired by Professor Robert Olin, call themselves. They have calculated that 10 to 20 per cent of the Swedish population may be suffering from sickness syndromes for which there are no recognized diagnoses. Though in a relatively sparsely populated part of Sweden, the network already has almost 700 members. Gertie Gladnikoff tells me that the national ME association is non-active as no one has the energy to keep it running. Those who are suffering from chronic fatigue can't manage to take care of their own interests. Currently discussions are being held about this network for people with different neurosomatic illnesses joining the long-established Swedish organization for the neurologically ill.

I asked: But won't you disappear without a trace in this organization? Isn't this exactly what the authorities want — that you will become invisible in tiny, separate organizations or disappear inside larger, established organizations that cover already recognized illnesses? Gertie Gladnikoff sighed:

> We hope, of course, that with the help of a larger organization we will get response to our demands for a reorganization of the medical services so that it can cater for today's complex illnesses. At present we are treated in an insulting manner and do not get adequate help.

In addition to Gertie Gladnikoff and Robert Olin, the writers of the article were Görel Thurdin, former Minister for the Environment, Birger Schlaug, Member of Parliament, the Green Party, Björn Regland and Vera Stejskal, university lecturers, and Britt-Inger Umefjord, a doctor. This important article was, as mentioned, published in one of the smaller dailies in Sweden. The writers had hoped that their message would become more widespread but, it seems, the major newspapers didn't wish to publish a debate article that was in exact opposition to the predominant thoughts on stress in working life as the major, perhaps the sole, cause of the catastrophically increasing ill-health.

Stress is, obviously, a problem nowadays and union demands for humane conditions in working life are highly justified. But more and more people have begun to realize that the new types of hypersensitivity and other forms of illness can hardly be fully explained by stress and poor organization of work.

"Other hypersensitivity" is a more official name for neurosomatic illnesses, given in Sweden as a heading for the different types of hypersensitivity that cannot be diagnosed as allergies triggered by known immunological mechanisms. In 1999, Folkhälsoinstitutet, the Swedish National Institute of Public Health, together with the Vårdal Trust, took the initiative for an inventory of the knowledge on these syndromes. The intention was to estimate the need for research and to find out which preventative measures could be taken.

A survey of the occurrence of multiple chemical sensitivity (MCS) in some European countries had been conducted by the EU as early as 1994. It was found that people in different countries and population groups reported the same type of symptoms, triggered by chemicals such as insecticides, solvents, paints, lacquers, and formaldehyde.

In Sweden, a survey of MCS and other syndromes was started much later. A working group, led by Professor Jan E. Wahlberg at the Clinic for Occupational Dermatology at Karolinska Hospital in Stockholm, made an inventory of the complaints that it was appropriate to include in what is also referred to as "special environmental sensitivity." The following were thought to be worth including in the environmental sensitivities: sick building syndrome, asthma-like symptoms, nettle rash, food intolerance, fibromyalgia, VDU-sickness, chronic fatigue syndrome, oral galvanism, MCS, non-specified hyper-reactions, skin complaints, non-allergic contact eczema, sensory hyper-reactivity, and electrosensitivity. The terms used are the group's own. They cause the reflection that the medical profession doesn't lack imagination when it comes to categorizing patients. But what do you do if one and the same patient has all the symptoms? If he, or she, is to be sent to all of the specialists involved, there is a risk that "multiple personality" must be added to the list.

Professor Jan E. Wahlberg had come across the problem with this type of hypersensitivity before he accepted this commission. In the 1980s his clinic had queues of patients with skin symptoms related to VDUs. These patients were probably never asked how they reacted to chemicals. Jan E. Wahlberg was irritated by them, complaining in interviews with journalists that they took time away from "more important" groups of patients. Even earlier, during the 1970s, he had had patients with skin and mucous membrane disorders arising from self-copying, or carbonless paper. He examined 150 patients but could not find any allergic reaction to this type of paper; he tells in an interview: "Over time the debate ebbed out, but a real hurricane was just around the corner, the VDU-sickness."

Self-copying paper, which contains formaldehyde and PCB, has disappeared from offices, so it is perhaps not so remarkable that the debate ebbed out. But there were researchers who found that this paper could give rise to skin symptoms and contribute to air pollution in offices. On the back of the first type of self-copying paper there was a thin coating of microcapsules that contained blue ink. This coloring was dissolved in PCB, polychlorinated biphenyls. When you wrote on the paper, the tiny capsules were crushed and a copy was made on the second sheet. Only a small portion of the capsules was utilized, the rest remaining on the back of the sheet. When these papers were stored, so was the PCB. When archives are cleared the papers may be sent to a paper mill for recycling. In this way, Professor Jan Rennerfelt warns, new quantities of PCB, which has been banned since 1976 in Sweden, may come into circulation. The problem with self-copying paper was not as negligible as Jan E. Wahlberg made out in interviews. No one has tried to get to the bottom of the stories that older female office workers often told. Later, some of these women had problems from VDUs; perhaps their "cup" of chemicals ran over. Jan E. Wahlberg's attitude to those who had become ill when working with VDUs is equally astonishing. Many of those who queued outside his clinic in the 1980s are still ill.

One of them is Kristina Fahlcrantz, who was sandwiched by different doctors' views in 1988. She had been Jan E. Wahlberg's patient for two years when she, as she puts it, "was thrown out of" the Clinic for Occupational Dermatology at Karolinska Hospital and referred to a psychologist. She was told that the changes in her skin, which had been verified by Björn Lagerholm, were only common changes due to ageing.

Under the microscope, Lagerholm, as well as another doctor in the dermatology clinic at Karolinska Hospital, had found that Kristina Fahlcrantz had external and intracellular edemas in the basal cell layers in the skin, greatly enlarged blood vessels and inflammation in her face, neck, and chest. The elastic fibers in her skin were also damaged. Moreover, she had an abnormally high number of mast cells, which, according to Björn Lagerholm, explained why she had burning and itching sensations in her skin.

Kristina Fahlcrantz became sick in 1982; for six months she had been working as an encoder, using a VDU from 9 to 5 each workday when she began to get a taste of metal in her mouth, and her skin was covered in red blotches. At the time, there was no debate on VDU operator skin complaints in Sweden. She was given other work for the next two years, but, in 1985, when she began working in front of an Ericsson Alfaskop screen, the skin complaints started again, this time even worse. Neither cortisone nor other allergy treatment tablets were of any help. Two years later she got a Siemens VDU. Now her hypersensitivity broke out in full force. She couldn't go near VDUs or fluorescent lights without feeling as if heat struck her. She had pains and numbness in her left cheek.

When I phoned Jan E. Wahlberg, to ask his opinion of the certificate written by his colleagues in the skin clinic of the hospital he was working at, he explained that he regarded the changes in Kristina Fahlcrantz's skin to be "normal for her age." She was 40. But, Jan E Wahlberg added that he wasn't a histopathologist; "it's possible that Björn Lagerholm has made a unique discovery, but as long as he hasn't presented what he has observed internationally and as no one else has been able to verify it, everything is up in the air."

Kristina Fahlcrantz never returned to work. She is one of the many victims in "the real hurricane" of the 1980s who queued up to see Jan E. Wahlberg.

At the end of the 1990s, the debate on multiple chemical sensitivity, MCS, reached Sweden in earnest. In reality, chemical hypersensitivity had been part of the picture with respect to those with chronic fatigue and/or electro-hypersensitivity all the time, but debates do have a tendency to be about one thing at a time. The complexity of various phenomena is seldom reflected.

To begin with, MCS was referred to as "smell sickness". But sensitivity to smelly substances is only one of the MCS symptoms defined in the USA. In addition it is often the case that people react to chemicals before they become aware of the smell. Judging by Swedish descriptions in the media, MCS seems to be a question of people who, quite suddenly, have become hypersensitive to the mere smell of somewhat harmless things like flowers and perfumes. Nowadays, of course, we know that perfumes are not as harmless as we had thought; there are reports that they contain phenols and artificial musk substances that are stored in the body. But perfumes don't draw attention to work environment hazards, which are hardly mentioned in this context.

In other countries, above all the US, it has been much more strongly emphasized that those afflicted by MCS may have been exposed to harmful doses of hazardous substances, and thereafter they have begun to react to various smells. Even though MCS is disputed in the US, Americans have, at least, discussed the importance that emissions from chemicals in, for example, different plastic products may have. It seems that this aspect continues to be swept under the carpet in Sweden. Many Swedish experts would rather talk about psychological conditioning. One of them, already mentioned, is Lena Hillert, doctor at a department for environmental sensitivity, where people who are electro-hypersensitive, chemically sensitive, or suffering from chronic fatigue or amalgam-related problems are dealt with. She explains that, under normal circumstances, the brain disregards smells other than that of fire or something similar. But, if one "switches on" the part of the brain that says you should be observant of something, "the result may be a general symptom pattern". Obviously her opinion is that it is a matter of conditioned reflexes. But, if you want to refer to the classic example of Pavlov's dogs, or people who are allergic to roses reacting to plastic roses, you ought to bear in mind that conditioned reflexes disappear after a rather short time.

Apparently, most American researchers who have studied the pattern of symptoms referred to as MCS, have abandoned the conditioned reflex hypothesis. It seems remarkable to me that the Swedish experts, who express themselves about the new sicknesses of hypersensitivity, do not pay more attention to another conceivable mechanism: as there are substances, like epoxy, that give rise to increasingly general hypersensitivity it cannot be ruled out that previous major or lengthy exposure to low doses may cause hypersensitivity. It is known that workers who have been injured by solvents are often extremely sensitive even to weak smells of similar substances, but when new occupational groups from office environments begin to complain of symptoms of this kind a psychological explanation is sought after, whilst no investigation is carried out into which chemicals they have been exposed to.

As Lena Hillert presents things, MCS is something that arises in an unknown manner and that the individuals affected can free themselves from, preferably with the help of experts in cognitive therapy. This therapy assumes that people can learn to live with, or "think away," their unpleasant symptoms. She has suggested that hypnosis, together with cognitive therapy, can be of partial help for some patients. She also mentions that medication, using beta-receptor blockers, could be suitable, without discussing the risks of such medicines and whether their use is justified at all in this context.

Lena Hillert's background includes working in a clinic for occupational and environmental medicine at Huddinge Hospital, outside Stockholm. Whilst there, in the 1990s, she was part of a research team working on what they called the electromagnetic field syndrome. That this syndrome was most similar to hypochondria was something the researchers made quite clear in their successful applications for funding. The actual aim of the project was quite simply to cure what the team regarded as an imaginary illness by using cognitive therapy. The vocabulary used by the team included "profit through sickness" – electro-hypersensitive patients were suspected of being sick to further their own material gain, or, perhaps in a desire to be noticed and taken care of.

One of the characteristics of the activities at Huddinge Hospital was that people who were seriously afflicted by hypersensitivity to electricity and chemicals were quickly sorted out and not given the treatment available. "You are a unique and difficult case, unfortunately we can't help you," they were told. The researchers concentrated their efforts on milder cases of skin complaints arising in connection with the use of VDUs, people who had not needed to be placed on the sick list for any length of time, perhaps not at all, but who were worried that their symptoms could develop into something more serious.

In an interview I conducted with Lena Hillert, I asked if she was prepared to draw parallels between patients suffering from electro-hypersensitivity and MCS, because it can be observed that sensitivity to chemicals has formed an important part of the symptoms reported by people suffering from hypersensitivity to electromagnetic radiation. "That isn't my experience," she answered. But what about those who have flame-retardants and other chemicals in their blood after working with VDUs?

> We still know very little about the effects chemicals could have, above all in relation to acute symptoms that those who are electrosensitive describe. I think it's a question of mixed groups. It could, of course, also be a question of a two-stage rocket in many of these groups. One could say that the more advanced the cases are and the longer people have been ill, the more similar the symptoms become.
>
> They differ in early phases, if you take someone who is electrosensitive, someone with MCS, and someone with symptoms related to amalgam. I think that we must go further and separate the different groups. As long as we bunch them all together on rather weak grounds, such as the individuals themselves having made the interpretation that they are electrosensitive, or hypersensitive to chemicals, we continue to risk failing to acquire knowledge by having groups that are too mixed.
>
> The groups have to be characterized; we need to find groups with similar symptoms and similar experience. Then, in these separate groups, we can investigate different backgrounds. You can look at how the symptoms first appeared, if the pattern of symptoms is similar, and so on.

But if you don't, for example, do blood analyses to see if there are flame-retardants or other chemicals, how can the groups be separated? To this question, Lena Hillert replied: "We could do the analyses, but as long as we haven't evaluated what this means it doesn't tell us anything."

This doesn't seem particularly logical to a layman. A research doctor, used as a Swedish and European expert on electro-hypersensitivity and other hypersensitivities, thinks that it is unnecessary to find out what chemicals the patients who come to her with undiagnosed symptoms have in their blood. She is right when saying that we don't yet know what health effects different levels of chemicals have. But, isn't it by collecting data of this kind that knowledge can be built up?

On the one hand she wants to take a comprehensive approach, on the other to survey those afflicted and divide them further. The criteria she talks about are so diffuse that one can suspect that childhood and life traumas the patients may have experienced could sooner or later be included here, precisely as they were earlier at Huddinge Hospital. In the end, each group will probably consist of a single individual. How will it then be possible to motivate public expenditure in the form of research and practical measures? Many experts may become occupied with labeling patients for the rest of their lives.

The interest seems to be focused on individual idiosyncrasies in general, and how one can use cognitive therapy to adapt individuals to the environment. Over a few legendary decades attempts were made in Sweden to adapt work environments to individuals instead. As an old journalist from a union journal, I remember and feel the loss of that era. Now commerce and industry are dictating terms, and researchers are taking part in scientific councils set up by and/or controlled by industry.

✖

Many of the chemicals that have come into common use since the Second World War are included in explanations of symptoms described by those who are hypersensitive to chemicals. Orga-nophosphates, used in insecticides and as flame-retardants and softening agents in plastics, are often mentioned in this context. When the EU began to take an interest in MCS, a problem of nomenclature arose. At a workshop in Berlin, organized by the WHO and others, it was decided to define this as "idiopathic environmental intolerances"; idiopathic defined as self-originated or of unknown causation. Self-defined illnesses are among the worst doctors can imagine. Patients are not supposed to diagnose things for themselves, nor say that they know what has caused their symptoms. What is interesting about this way of defining MCS, as agreed in Berlin, is that the main sponsor for the meeting was an organization called The International Program on Chemical Safety (PPCS), which is regarded as being close to the chemical industry. Most of the participants represented this industry. It is quite natural that manufacturers of all kinds wish to have MCS and other syndromes regarded as occurring from unknown causes, not from their products. But it is more difficult to understand the lack of interest in this question shown by public authorities.

Cindy Duehring, an American medical student who was awarded the alternative Nobel Prize – the Right Livelihood Award – in 1997, has written that never before in the history of mankind have we had such a global epidemic that has been ignored by the authorities. She became hypersensitive to almost everything, including electromagnetic fields, following a large dose of insecticides that were used to combat insects in her apartment. She couldn't watch TV without having painful attacks. She pointed out the many different names used for this epidemic in different countries and how many categories of people had been affected by this illness, whose symptoms are triggered by very low amounts of a multitude of different chemicals.

"There is a similarity across those afflicted in all countries and there are debates everywhere between doctors who believe that it is chemicals that trigger the illness and those who believe that it is a question of psychogenic mass epidemics," Cindy Duehring wrote, in the speech that a friend of hers read on her behalf in connection with the Award. She was unable to collect the prize herself, as she was too weak and hypersensitive. She died recently. Towards the end she couldn't even tolerate sounds.

Claudia Miller is another person who has been active in the American MCS debate. She is a researcher at the University of Texas Health Science Center in San Antonio. In her opinion hypersensitivity occurs in two stages. First come symptoms related to a sick building or a workplace with chemical emissions of different kinds. For some reason we completely lose tolerance for that which we have been exposed to. In the next phase we develop hypersensitivity to other substances. Now reaction occurs even to very small doses. She calls this loss of toxic tolerance.

She has noted that the most serious symptoms of MCS have been reported by people who have been exposed to organophosphates, present in many chemical pesticides. She also points out that chemicals, such as flame-retardants called poly-brominated biphenyls, PBB, and trichloro-ethylene can attack both the nervous and the immune systems. One compound, Bromex – used in Sweden against fur beetles – has been named in this context by electro-hypersensitive Swedes. According to information, Bromex has been banned since 1990. It is an organophosphate compound with bromide, which, when inhaled, can cause serious symptoms. Like other organophosphates, Bromex is easily absorbed by the skin. The toxic effect of the substance is raised by heat, visible light and UV light.

I note, once again, this is a mechanism that occurs in various contexts concerning chemicals: their interaction with heat and UV, or even visible light. We know, in addition, that microwaves can increase the speed of chemical reactions. As yet, I have not read a single official Swedish research report, dissertation, or debate article about electro-hypersensitivity that has touched on these combinations. But there must be a number of chemists and other experts who are aware of these mechanisms and reflect over the fact that they take place in connection with all our electrical devices.

It is believed that loss of toxic tolerance of the kind that Claudia Miller talks about has been identified in American and British soldiers who took part in the Gulf War in 1990–1991. Since the war they have had chronic symptoms that are very much like those of MCS and other syndromes. They have developed chemical hypersensitivity towards a successively increasing number of substances but also, for example, light hypersensitivity and chronic fatigue.

Professor Emeritus Robert Olin, one of the co-signers of the article mentioned at the beginning of this chapter, describes the Gulf War Syndrome in a publication about neurosomatic illnesses, published by Nationella Folkhälsokommittén, the National Public Health Committee in Sweden. About 50,000 (sometimes the figure mentioned is 100,000) of the 700,000 soldiers who had been stationed in Saudi Arabia were afflicted by a multifaceted pattern of illness less than six months after the Gulf War. The pattern included muscle and joint complaints, lowered intellectual capacity, and unspecified neurological symptoms. Robert Olin writes that the toxic effects of the chemical substances they were exposed to have not been confirmed, but that the suspicion remains. During the Gulf War, soldiers had been given a preventative medicine called pyridostigminbromide, as well as numerous vaccinations and preventative medicines for nerve gases. The medicine is believed to have caused abnormal levels of the nerve signal substance acetylcholine, which has an effect on many different body functions such as sleep, muscle activity, memory, and the sensation of pain. It transmits messages between nerve cells or from nerve cells to muscle cells. The concentration of acetylcholine is regulated by two enzymes, acetylcholinesterase and butyrylcholinesterase; if these enzymes are inhibited the level of acetylcholine can become too high.

The nerve gas, sarin, together with, for example, various in-secticides, belongs to the group of organophosphates that can disturb enzyme functions. It is suspected that soldiers were exposed to this dangerous chemical when a factory in Kuwait was blown up. Insecticides were spread in areas where the soldiers were stationed. According to one hypothesis, the soldiers were simply overloaded with chemicals, including organophosphates, which, in some cases, strengthened the effect of each other. What Robert Olin does not mention is that suspicions have also been raised about the microwaves that the soldiers were exposed to. This is especially interesting when one thinks of the repeated animal experiments in Sweden (see Chapter 10) that have clearly shown that microwaves open the blood–brain barrier in rats so that poisons can enter the brain from the blood.

The Pentagon has published a report in which a presentation of the chemical hypothesis is given. In this report the suspicion is also put forward that stress, too, could have contributed to penetration of pyridostigminbromide from the blood into the brain. In this case, stress can be seen as a paraphrase for microwaves, whose ability to open the blood–brain barrier gives rise to such considerable concern that the Pentagon can be expected to want to express itself cautiously.

After the Gulf War Syndrome came the Balkan Syndrome. It was reported that UN soldiers who served in places like Bosnia in 1994–1995 had similar multifaceted symptoms to the Gulf soldiers, including pain in muscles and joints, skin complaints, throat ache, numbness, respiratory problems, digestive problems, and sleep disturbances as well as concentration and memory loss.

Later, the debate was concentrated on whether depleted uranium, which had been used in projectiles and missiles both in Bosnia and in the Kosovo War in 1999, could have caused cases of leukemia reported among the soldiers. This connection was refuted by the experts: the concentrations of radioactive plutonium found in ammunition were said to be far too low to cause cases of leukemia.

On the other hand, there were people who pointed out that the chemicals in the uranium dust as well as the smoke from the burning oil wells in Kuwait could have been a greater danger. Various experts tried to insist that it was only a psychological phenomenon. These experts were, however, in the minority; most of those who studied the problem agreed that it could not be explained in psychological terms.

In the journal *New Scientist* there was a report in March 2003 about a breakthrough in the research about the Gulf war Syndrome. It was officially admitted that stress could not be the explanation for the fact that there was 30 per cent more sick people among the Gulf veterans than among comparable groups. It was shown with magnetic resonance spectroscopy (MRS) that in people with serious problems, such as confusion and dizziness, nerve cells had disappeared in the basal ganglia; structures involved in brain functions were disturbed in those with the syndrome.

I came into early contact with people who aroused suspicions that radio frequencies and chemicals could have interactive effects. One of them was Bertil Arting, a teacher and radio ham who lives in Bollnäs, 250 km north of Stockholm. He became so hypersensitive to electromagnetic fields that he could sense VDUs and TVs through walls and floors. Earlier he had been the amateur radio champion in Sweden; now he can no longer stand being close to any kind of radio transmitter, wireless microphone, cellular phone, electric tool, or domestic machine. He and his wife live in a highly adapted house in a forest, far away from neighbors. In his own words:

> I got my ham license in the 1950s. On the HF bands, such as SM3VE, I accomplished nearly a quarter of a million two-way contacts, mainly using high-speed telegraphy but also AM, SSB, and radio teletype. My transmitters were powerful, 1 kW. From 1971 to 1987 we lived 40 meters from a 220 kV power line.

In addition, in the mid 1970s, I started talking to local friends, using the 145 MHz waveband running 10 watts to an indoor antenna on my work desk. The antenna was half a meter from my head. In this way, I was exposed to a fairly strong field of radiation of a relatively high frequency. My large HF transmitter gave stronger fields but on lower frequencies. From time to time I used an unshielded antenna tuner on those lower frequencies.

At the same time, the mid 1970s, I was poisoned by photographic fixing fluid, Kodak F 24. I spilled five liters of fluid on a wall-to-wall carpet in my darkroom. When I had finally succeeded in drying everything out, I had breathed in so much of the toxic fumes that my sight was impaired – my field of vision became minimal. I saw everything in a haze and fell very ill.

After this happened, I became hypersensitive to chemical substances in the air – paints, sprays, perfumes, deodorants, tobacco smoke, petrol fumes, etc. When things were at their worst, I had partial loss of memory, difficulties in finding words, and problems with speech, sight, and balance. I want to emphasize that I am mentally strong and stable.

I gradually became better, but the symptoms came back almost every time I sat at my work desk.

Routine allergy tests revealed nothing. When the symptoms didn't disappear Bertil Arting began a systematic investigation of his environment. He took out the flowers from the room but it didn't help. The only things left were his typewriter and a table lamp. When he leaned forward over the lamp he felt a slight smell of something burnt. The lamp socket, which was made of white bakelite, had a nasty brown discoloring, caused by heat from the light bulb. Bakelite was the first plastic, a combination of phenol and formaldehyde. From the 1930s it was used in cases for electrical goods, telephones, door handles, ashtrays, pipes, etc. Formaldehyde is also a common component in developing fluids. It is corrosive and poisonous when inhaled; it reacts chemically, bonding with proteins in the body as well as DNA, which may give rise to damaged chromosomes, a first step towards cancer. Other information on formaldehyde is that it bonds into the respiratory system and also superficially, in the eyes, causing great damage. It also causes skin allergies. Examination of workers who have been exposed to formaldehyde, showed that 10 per cent of them had chest pressure and breathing difficulties.

For some time, Bertil Arting thought he had found the problem, that it was the lamp socket, but he didn't immediately think of the fact that he had not operated his 145 MHz radio at all for several days. As soon as he started using the transceiver again, the symptoms came back. After some experiments he proved to himself that radiation from the antenna affected him. To cut a long story short, over the years, Bertil Arting has seen his hypersensitivity increase. In 1994 he had to give up teaching as he had a recurring heart condition that got worse as the years went by.

He is by no means a unique case. Radio amateur colleagues have experienced similar symptoms. They were early in becoming concerned about the development of mobile telephony, but few were prepared to listen to their warnings.

Dust particles, with hazardous content, are drawn to VDUs, TV sets, and the surfaces of other electrical devices. As a research team at Helsinki University in Finland has discovered, poisons are absorbed into plastic materials and plasterboard, and remain there for a long time. These researchers don't discuss electrical devices, but anyone can draw conclusions when we know that the static and alternating electric fields in various devices attract all airborne particles. Once again, this shows how unsuitable the combination of plastics and devices that produce heat and electrical fields can be.

The Finnish research team, led by Professor Mirja Salkinoja-Salonen, have identified about 10 bacteria, which can explain health problems arising from sick buildings. These bacteria create what are known as mitochondria toxins, which are deposited everywhere and can give rise to the different symptoms that are usually found in descriptions of sick building syndrome. These poisons have an adverse effect on energy production in some structures of the cells, called mitochondria. They may even lead to early ageing. The bacteria multiply extremely quickly, especially in buildings that have been damaged by water.

Anna, a teacher in Gothenburg, has had a chain of illness that is of interest in this context. Her problems started in 1989 when she was working in a school that had major problems with mold. Her classroom had been sprayed with fungicides in 1987. The problem with mildew didn't disappear. In 1989, the roof started to leak and the walls and ceiling became damp. The floor also became damp, as the base of the building was directly on the ground. The entire staff in the school had different symptoms – fatigue, headaches, concentration difficulties, mucous membrane complaints, and infections of various kinds. At first, Anna's symptoms disappeared when she was at home, but came back when she returned to work. After having pneumonia in 1991, she has had permanent problems. She has become increasingly sensitive to things that hadn't affected her earlier. She was put on the sick list, the diagnosis being chronic fatigue, or alternatively sick building sickness. Her claim for occupational injuries compensation was approved. Nowadays, Anna also reacts to fluorescent lighting, low-energy lamps, computers, mobile phones and similar devices.

> I get acute symptoms such as dizziness, muzziness, and a feeling of not being here, as well as eye irritations, muscle strain, and a fast pulse. In some environments I feel a kind of asthma. I've also become sensitive to alcohol and coffee and react against an increasing number of foods.

Swedish experts whose task is to get a comprehensive overview of the new illnesses have given an account of their view in the 2001 publication, *From Witchcraft to Science*. This publication can be said to be an inventory of the symptoms that occur, but these experts are wary of dealing with the issue of causal connections.

The person who is perhaps the most concrete is Professor Jan Sundell from the International Center for Indoor Environment and Energy at the Technical University of Denmark. He has been an expert on "sick buildings" for many years, but admits that research hasn't got very far. It is not known, he writes, whether the symptoms that are usually reported as being sick building syndrome, SBS, are of one single syndrome, or several different ones.

He points out that it is difficult to draw the line between SBS, multiple chemical sensitivity, and the chronic fatigue and immune dysfunction syndrome. He also mentions electro-hypersensitivity as a contributory symptom in this context. "At the beginning of the 1980s the idea was to dismiss SBS as a mass psychogenic illness, but several epidemiological studies have shown correlations to objective environmental factors, such as the type of building, ventilation, copying machines, working with VDUs, handling paper, lighting, and dampness/ mold," he writes.

At present Sweden has the highest level of long-term sickness in the EU. In this welfare state, with one of the best developed social security systems in the world, and with strong and effective trade unions that look after workers' rights, the number of employees reporting sick is increasing daily. It has been calculated that the costs of ill health are increasing by three million euros per day. This sum is three times greater than the national expenditure on schools and education. The sickness bomb is a catastrophe.

Why do people become ill in a country in which traditional work environment risks have been dealt with over many years? In this context one might expect a debate about the role of various new environmental factors. But no. Instead, experts in psychosocial matters and stress have become the nation's gurus. The mass media excels in portraying people who have been forced to take sick leave or early retirement because of stress or burnout. Some experts draw parallels with hysteria among women in earlier centuries. Great attention is paid to such experts and they are awarded prizes. But the number of those on the sick list continues to rise.

Questioning our modern environment is taboo.

16

Outcasts in Nokia country

A Finn ought to be able to stand a little radiation! That's the general opinion in Finland, especially after Nokia's successes.

In this country, which had the highest density of mobile phones in the world over a long period, there is hardly any debate about the health risks of microwaves. Even less is discussed about risks connected to chemicals in electronics. Nearly every schoolchild owns a mobile phone. Nokia directs marketing to this group, without bothering about warnings given by researchers that children's brains ought not to be exposed to microwaves from cell phones, a warning that has been heeded in countries such as the UK and Germany. The only issues Finnish media have discussed are that the masts used for mobile telephony spoil the countryside from an aesthetic point of view, and that telephone calls disturb classroom concentration.

Nokia is the golden calf. A certain amount of humility is expected with respect to the demands that Nokia makes on the Finnish community as a condition for remaining in the country. Prior to the fall of the Soviet Union, when Finland was politically obliged to adapt to "the great neighbor to the East," the Germans talked about "Finlandisierung." An analogy with this could be to speak of a "Nokialisierung," as one Finnish debater put it. There were those who would rather have seen Jorma Ollila, Nokia's

CEO, as the country's President instead of Tarja Halonen, but he declined to run for office. He has more power as it is.

So, it isn't surprising that the general public in Finland is unaware that some foreign researchers are following developments with great interest, asking the question: will the high density of mobile phones lead to world record numbers suffering from Alzheimer's, Parkinson's, and cancer, too? Finnish media give scant coverage to alarming research results that may have an effect on Nokia's legendary success. Today, every third mobile phone in the world is a Nokia.

Living in such a technologically highly developed country, it is just not done to say that you get sick when using computers, not to mention mobile phones. To do so is asking to be ostracized. Bengt Mether, 49, has experienced this. He has a university education in the field of computers, his main subject being information processing, which he studied at Åbo Academy. Early in his career he developed systems for PCs and began to develop programs at IBM in 1976. For almost 20 years he ran his own consultancy in the field of computerization – in other words he was a successful businessman in an area that was given the highest priority in Finland. But, whilst using computers, he became afflicted by the same symptoms as so many others around the world. At first it was his sight that got worse and worse. It didn't help when he was operated on to have new lenses in his eyes. After a while he was told that he had cataracts. But it wasn't just his eyes. He got rashes and reddening in the face. His skin became so sensitive that he could hardly shave. "It stung and burned all over my face, except under my chin. I thought I'd become allergic and tried using a lot of different ointments but they didn't help." But more than anything else it was the tiredness that bothered him, a tiredness that had made him reduce his working hours. Sometimes he couldn't raise enough energy to go home by public transport so he took a taxi. It became increasingly difficult to concentrate and he had memory blackouts. He convinced himself that it was simply stress.

In 1999 I became so chronically ill that I couldn't do the work
that I'd promised clients. I thought that all my senses had become hypersensitive in some way; I reacted to light, sound, and
touch and had a very low pain threshold. My sight continued to
get worse and worse.

At that stage, Bengt Mether heard about an association for
electro-hypersensitive people in Finland. When he met some of
the members of this association it was somewhat of a revelation;
everyone had the same symptoms that he had. Most of them also
had similar backgrounds. That was how he, a person who had
never before heard the term electro-hypersensitivity, got involved
in the activities of the association. He soon became frustrated
by the attitude of most doctors when he mentioned the word
electro-hypersensitivity. His family doctor realized he was ill but
was unable to give a diagnosis. In order, at least, to exclude the
possibility of a tumor, or something similar, the doctor referred
Bengt Mether to a neurologist. But, in the referral it was stated,
"the patient thinks he is suffering from electro-hypersensitivity".
The neurologist carried out a short examination, tapped Bengt
Mether's knees and explained that he didn't believe that there was
such a thing as electro-hypersensitivity; "you don't mind if I refer
you to a psychiatrist, do you?"

That's the state of affairs at the time of writing. He has a
non-existent illness. KELA, the Finnish authority that manages
payment of sickness allowance and pensions, has a list of illnesses
that are "approved" and electro-hypersensitivity is not included.
The diagnosis is not accepted in Sweden either, but if a person
in Sweden has such serious symptoms that he/she cannot work
sickness allowance is paid out in almost all cases. This is not so
in Finland where KELA categorically refuse to pay. Over the years,
many people, who have become ill whilst using VDUs, have been
referred to KELA hospitals for examination. Their fate has always
been the same; a short examination, a few comforting words that
nothing is wrong and a referral to a psychiatrist. "I believe it is a

conscious, agreed policy," says Bengt Mether.

> They want us to accept a psychological diagnosis and be re-
> warded with sickness allowance or a pension. Then they can
> refer to statistics and say, "you see, there is no such thing as
> electro-hypersensitivity, they've imagined everything."

The shock of seeing new sides of the community in which he
previously lived a privileged life made Bengt Mether become
active in the association for electro-hypersensitive people, which
has just over 500 members. He has visited authorities and trade
unions to inform them about the situation, but has been met by a
deprecatory attitude that has made him deeply upset.

> It is clear that the policy in the country coincides with the in-
> terests of big business. This is reflected throughout the whole
> of society down to the individual officials who make decisions.
> Perhaps these marionettes sometimes act in good faith.

Not even the Finnish trade unions have bothered that so many of
their members have become sick when using computers. Union
officials don't want to concern themselves with the issue. Bengt
Mether has met the same indifferent attitude in trade unionists,
doctors, and public authorities. He knows that it was a VDU that
triggered his symptoms. He is typical for this group in Finland.
A questionnaire, answered by members of the association, shows
that office workers, above all from the IT sector, are in the majority
in the group. Approximately 90 per cent got their first symptoms
in front of VDUs, a smaller number when using mobile phones.
But, often, those who became ill whilst using VDUs, can't tolerate
using cell phones.

Exposure to the type of chemicals found in electronics is, of course,
of current interest for groups other than office workers who use

computers. It is not uncommon to meet workers who have been exposed to epoxy for example. Two such cases are described below. They have both been diagnosed as hypersensitive to light, so doctors take them seriously and no one questions their right to receive sickness allowance.

Esko Puuperä, 55, had been an electrical fitter at Kemira in Oulu, northern Finland, for 27 years when he was forced to stop working because of severe hypersensitivity to light. It began in 1991, with rashes on his legs. To begin with he was given light treatment on his entire body in a solarium used by a private doctor. The result was catastrophic. It felt as if his skin burned, he told me. Later he came to a hospital. Here, too, he was given light treatment intermittently with cortisone injections. It wasn't until 1993 that a senior nurse put forward the hypothesis that he was suffering from light sensitivity. In 1995 he was given a final diagnosis: Polymorphic hypersensitivity to light, i.e. sensitivity to different kinds of light. Above all it is UV-A that he cannot tolerate and has to protect himself against. Fluorescent tubes, in shops and public buildings, give rise to symptoms. Even on cloudy days he finds it difficult to be outdoors. He always keeps the blinds drawn in his apartment. He is, however, able to move around outdoors, using his car, fitted with sunscreens of the type used in shop windows to protect goods from sunlight. They don't allow the long-wave UV-A radiation to get through. It was rather difficult to find the right kind of screening, as there are strict regulations that the windows of cars may not be fitted with anything that restricts visibility.

When Esko Puuperä has been examined by different doctors there hasn't been much discussion of what work he has done. He is rather surprised at the lack of curiosity on the part of doctors to find out what he has been exposed to at work, but he thinks this may be because of general reticence to get involved in conflicts. Starting an occupational injuries process isn't all that easy in Finland. Insurance company lawyers and medical specialists do their best to deny any claim that something in the work environment has caused an illness.

He has told doctors that he has handled a great deal of epoxy adhesives and been exposed to epoxy fumes. As has been noted many times earlier in this book, there are scientific reports that substances formed when epoxy decomposes can cause chronic hypersensitivity to light. Bearing this in mind it was an outrageous error of judgment to put Esko Puuperä in a solarium, exposing him to the very thing that he had become hypersensitive to! Doctors often lack sufficient knowledge about the hazards of chemicals. When they don't understand why patients react as they do doctors bury their own heads in the sand.

Esko Puuperä has been exposed to quantities of other chemicals, too. On two occasions he has been close to an exploding capacitor, filled with PCB, polychlorinated biphenyls. PCB was splattered on the walls and he had to clean up afterwards.

Another Finn, Kari Koso, 36 years old, has also been exposed to epoxy whilst handling fillers and paints. He runs a transport company and drives lorries. Now he is facing early retirement; his hypersensitivity to light is a severe handicap. Like Esko Puuperä he reacts primarily to UV-A. But, in addition, he has begun to get symptoms from different electrical and electronic devices such as mobile phones, computers, drills, and vacuum cleaners. As far as I can understand, this may be very important. A person, who has been diagnosed as hypersensitive to light, may consequently react to other forms of electromagnetic radiation.

If Kari Koso is exposed to sunlight through a closed car window he immediately gets symptoms, but if the window is open the symptoms – swellings and redness – appéar after some delay, usually a few hours. His skin has become increasingly sensitive to all forms of touch. He is hypersensitive to heat and cold. He cannot even stand eating warm food.

"It has to be cold and cloudy, otherwise I can't come to meet you!" I got this somewhat surprising message one summer, some years ago, when I was going to meet Virpi Leinonen, a journalist and artist. I had arranged to meet her at a place where some of her works of art were being shown in a major exhibition of Finnish modern art. She had told me that she was hypersensitive to light and electricity and that she had successively become sensitive to a number of chemicals, too.

Summer days in Finland can often be gray and cold. Luckily it was such a day. Virpi Leinonen turned up. After that first meeting, we've met several times and exchanged letters. I have often understood that merely writing a letter is a physical exertion for her. "I have to carry things through by mobilizing my mental energy, then I have to rest up the following day," she once wrote in a letter.

Today, her life, in the countryside of the Finnish lake lands, is completely different from that she led only a few years ago. At that time she was a sought-after fashion editor and writer, reporting from the major fashion shows in Europe. She had written a book on textile art that has been translated into Swedish and published by the largest publishing house in Sweden.

She bought a new PC in 1989 and got eye and heart symptoms, feeling sick when in front of her VDU.

> No one could tell me what it was all about, so I constructed technical aids myself so that I could stand using it. I placed a thick acrylic sheet between the screen and myself. This helped against the eye complaints.

In connection with studying at university, she attended a computer course, sitting in a small room with 20 VDUs, a room full of fluorescent tubes in the ceiling. Soon she could no longer stand the light from the tubes, "the pain was unbearable". Her hypersensitivity now became permanent and the range of symptoms spread. It appears as though exposure in the computer room had functioned as a severely aggravating factor. Earlier, she had felt similar symptoms from fluorescent tubes. She became surprisingly weary in places lit by fluorescent lighting and used to get heart symptoms, sight problems, and headaches.

> My hypersensitivity didn't start with visible skin changes. I got heat spots in my scalp when I was close to fluorescent lighting. When my face became "burned" for the first time, I already had developed hypersensitivity, after that my skin began to react even to chemicals and dust in the air.

She used to seek out shady and cool places. Heart symptoms followed her reactions to light. These were triggered by the sun but went away in shade. Sunlight and hot water made her sick. Earlier she had loved being outside in the sun and warmth. Later, she came to have periods of extremely severe light hypersensitivity, during which even the daylight indoors and the light of Finnish summer nights was hard to bear. Neither clothes not sunglasses helped, "my skin felt pain from both light and heat".

> So, I've become successively sensitive to practically everything around me, chemicals, food, medicines... Many summers and winters have been spent indoors, behind dark curtains. In 1991, practically all light became unbearable. Sometimes I felt a little better, then a catastrophe struck me again. My eyes began to "burn" immediately if I happened to come into contact with sunlight during these most difficult periods. The following day I couldn't even look at white paper.

During the years that have gone by, Virpi Leinonen has still managed to produce some works of art. Mustering all the powers that she has left, she has produced works for exhibitions, like the ones she showed me several years ago. Working with light and darkness, she has tried to portray her experience of being "without skin, without eyelids". On the opening days of her own exhibitions she has been present, "standing under lamps, talking and laughing with everyone else, even if I was in terrible pain". She paid the price later, and has learned to judge how much exposure she can stand in a month, a year, etc.

From time to time she has even found the energy to take part in the debate, which the association for electro-hypersensitive people has attempted to arouse in Finland. In correspondence with me, she has often discussed the possibility of there being subgroups among those who refer to themselves as electro-hypersensitive.

She recognizes a lot of that which describes the chronic fatigue and immune dysfunction syndrome, CFIDS, in her own experience. CFIDS seems to have been unknown until the beginning of the 1980s, in any case as a term used for a specific clinical picture. There was almost an epidemic development in the USA at that time. Or was it a case of a group of doctors, who began to take an interest in this complex of symptoms? These doctors didn't, in any case, find a great deal of sympathy from those in authority, despite identifying ill-health deviations in their patients. The US Center of Disease coined the expression "chronic fatigue syndrome". CFIDS is linked with almost identical symptoms as multiple chemical sensitivity, MCS. The symptoms are also similar to those of electro-hypersensitivity and those arising in connection with sick building syndrome, SBS. Isn't it a question of the same sickness? No, says Virpi Leinonen. "The symptoms overlap, but it isn't a question of identical clinical pictures. On the other hand, the different groups have not undergone identical examinations."

A group of Finns who had VDU-related illnesses formed an association in the mid-1990s. To begin with, they concerned themselves with mutual help and advice rather than influencing public opinion. This made it possible for the authorities to ignore their problems. The only initiative taken by authorities is a minor survey of the symptoms of about 30 people. The Finnish Institute of Occupational Health produced this report about 10 years ago. It was noted that the same symptoms had been reported in Sweden, but this did not lead to any measures being taken. The Institute had early knowledge of the problem in question, but referred to researchers in Sweden who had not been able to establish what electro-hypersensitivity was.

It is completely clear that the Finnish authorities have been determined that the "infection" from Sweden, where the debate has been ongoing since 1985, should not catch on. A few years ago, journalists who phoned to the Institute of Occupational Health were told that the problem was not known in Finland, apart from on the west coast, where the Swedish-speaking population, who keep up with media reports from Sweden, live. But the problem has been known since the beginning of the 1980s and is equally widespread in both language communities in Finland.

As there has been no real research in Finland into this phenomenon, officials in Finnish authorities have reported to their counterparts in Sweden that "the phenomenon is not known in Finland". That both the Institute of Occupational Health and KELA have had hundreds of cases under investigation hasn't altered official reports; individuals are not counted until they are included in a scientific report or a diagnosis register.

Commencing in 2000, the association for electro-hypersensitive people in Finland has acquired the nature of a militant group that the authorities can no longer ignore. The current chairman, Matti Wirmaneva, is an electro-engineer but has also studied medicine. He does not have any hypersensitivity problems himself.

Through articles in the Finnish press , Erja Tamminen, the current information officer for the association, has made the problem known to a wider public. She worked as an information officer in a major Finnish company where she became ill. When representatives of various authorities have given sweeping excuses and calming information, she has provided them with the latest international research findings and demanded concrete answers: What measures do you intend to take as a consequence of this? It is becoming increasingly difficult for Finnish authorities to turn a blind eye to the problem.

Erja Tamminen has also collated facts in a book published

in 2002. The title in Finnish is *Sähköä ilmassa,* which means "Electricity in the air." This is the first book published in Finland that raises such matters.

In Finland there is no interest whatsoever in conducting research into the chronic symptoms referred to as electro-hypersensitivity despite Erja Tamminen's and others' attempts to encourage Finnish researchers to find out about the combined effects of electricity and chemicals. They continue to refer to the fact that Swedish researchers "haven't found anything" even though such intra-disciplinary research has never been carried out in Sweden.

One the other hand, quite a lot of research into the biological effects of electromagnetic fields is going on in Finland, among other research into the microwave spectrum. For example, in 2003 cell studies in Finland gave results that should cause concern but no debate arose in the country.

17

TCO-labeling and the zero risk goal

Low dose exposure to chemicals and electromagnetic radiation from increasingly advanced electronic equipment is apparently one of the work environment risks in offices in the twenty-first century. How great the health hazards are is not yet known. Researchers who want to find out are kept back by constant lack of funding. In this situation, the role of unions is important, partly with respect to demanding more adequate research in this field, partly to assert at least the principle of prudent avoidance – if they don't dare to demand a zero-risk goal.

TCO, the Swedish Confederation of Professional Employees, with 1.2 million members, is known around the world for its environmental labeling of computer display units, a guarantee that the electromagnetic fields have been reduced and that the worst chemicals are not present, at least not in the casings. This is a step in the right direction, but even the TCO label does not guarantee VDUs are harmless, as many who have become ill whilst using TCO-labeled screens have bitterly experienced.

But what is most remarkable is that TCO has shown that union members, as consumers, can place demands on manufacturers and influence them. Companies around the world understood early that the Swedish requirements would become the market standard and did their best to comply. Today, millions of people around the world are using TCO-certified computer screens. Almost half the screens that are being manufactured in the world are TCO-labeled. One reason for labeling to come about was that the Swedish work environment authorities were too dilatory with respect to their responsibility to check products and influence manufacturers. So, TCO took matters into their own hands to safeguard the interests of members. Many members were worried as early as the beginning of the 1980s, when discussions took place about the clusters of miscarriages among women who used VDUs at work. In 1985, a heated debate about VDU-related skin complaints followed. TCO maintained that the prudent avoidance principle should apply and that risks should be eliminated as far as possible.

Now, environmental labeling of mobile phones is beginning to take place. But there, TCO was late on the uptake, far behind, in the wake of the debate and alarming research reports on microwaves. One major reason for this lethargy is that the person behind TCO-labeling of screens, Per-Eric Boivie, was out-maneuvered by the former head of the TCO, Inger Ohlsson. She has said that she didn't like the TCO-label becoming an international success because people began to think that TCO was a test laboratory for VDUs, not a trade union! So, when Per-Erik Boivie wanted to extend the labeling to include mobile phones, at the end of the 1990s, he was given the "thumbs down" by the TCO Executive Committee at that time. "Don't come with new ideas," he was told. The mobile telephony industry could continue selling its products without interference.

When TCO-labeling for computer display units was introduced, the Finnish Nokia was the first to have their products labeled and to use this as an important sales argument for the company. Then, Nokia went completely over to producing mobile phones, unperturbed by concerns about health risks when no strong pressure group put forward demands. Worker protection and radiation protection authorities proved, once again, that they were completely powerless to act.

After electing a new chairman, TCO has now put forward requirements for certification of mobile phones, once again a world first, even if they are late this time. TCO has fixed the SAR value, the highest permissible radiation value, to 0.8 watt/kg. This means a lowering of the SAR value compared with the EU level, set at 2.0.

TCO is also launching a new method of taking measurements, called TCP, Telephone Communication Power, which indicates how much of the cell phone's radiation effect is really used for communication. Measurements have shown that up to 84 per cent of the microwaves from many mobile phones disappear into the heads of users!

TCO requires that mobile phones must not contain mercury, cadmium, lead, or beryllium. With respect to flame-retardants, the TCO requirement is that plastic components weighing more than 10 grams must not contain flame-retardants using organically bound chlorine or bromine.

Per-Erik Boivie was early to realize that chemicals in electronics would become an important issue. For the TCO "95 VDU Label" requirements were made that neither chlorinated nor brominated flame-retardants should be used in casings around devices. In this way, TCO has contributed to the almost complete disappearance of the use of poly-brominated diphenyl-ethers, PBDE, from at least casings. But there are also PBDEs in components inside the electronics.

No alternative has, however, been found to replace the brominated flame-retardant Tetrabromobisphenol-A, TBBPA, in circuit cards and small components. Here, TCO has taken the approach of not demanding something that manufacturers have not yet had the chance of complying with. One of those who have not backed this strategy is Bruno Hagi, an ombudsman at SIF, the Union of Clerical and Technical Employees in Industry, the largest union under the TCO umbrella. Together with experts, he had set up SIF's "Zero Risk Goal", which means that there should be no substances whatsoever in computers and other products that are harmful to people and the environment, if manufacturers want to have certification of their products. If they are unable to comply with this requirement, they should indicate this on the product in question. A surprising number of manufacturers agreed with him and were of the opinion that a zero risk goal is necessary to hasten developments. However, TCO as a whole was more doubtful.

Bruno Hagi also raised the requirement that high-frequency radiation should be eliminated from devices. He issued a warning that radiation was increasing in offices. When he alerted people about the continuous radiation from cordless (DECT) phones in the 1990s, the local SIF branch at Ericsson challenged his view. These phones were a major Ericsson product. This, in a nutshell, illustrated the unions' dilemma – the conflict between employment and health. Bruno Hagi explained that his ambition was to create more jobs in the industry. Strengthened user and environmental requirements contribute to product development and, in the long run, are advantageous for the export industry, he maintained.

Bruno Hagi is not an ombudsman at SIF anymore. His visions for a better work environment were not welcome. The leadership in the union emphasizes psychosocial problems at workplaces. The "burnout syndrome" is on everyone's lips. Psychologists and stress experts are presenting their solutions to the unions and sharing the members' money.

18

Electronic waste disposal

Electronic scrap is one of the major waste disposal problems in modern communities. For a long time now we have not known how to deal with it. If devices weren't simply thrown away on rubbish dumps just as they were, then expensive metals were removed and the rest ground down prior to dumping.

In this way, lead, PCB, chlorinated and brominated flame-retardants, mercury, nickel, cadmium, and many other substances were released into our environment and the eco cycle. Cathode ray tubes from computer screens and TV sets were crushed so that the strontium and beryllium baked into the glass was washed into the groundwater by rainfall. Strontium 89, found in this context, has been used as luminescent material on the inside of the glass in cathode ray tubes. It is counted as a less serious environmental poison, but gives off beta-radiation.

Even lead, lead oxide, and barium are found in the glass of cathode ray tubes. Beryllium, a metal classed as a poison, and its compounds, like barium and its compounds, are highly poisonous and can give rise to symptoms of illness after a short exposure time. A combination of barium and strontium is regarded as being extremely harmful. There are two types of glass in cathode ray tubes. The front glass contains barium as well as a certain amount of lead. The rear glass can contain up to 25 per cent lead. Swedish law does not permit such cathode ray tubes to be manufactured in Sweden; they have been imported from different Asian countries in which work environment laws are not so strict. Lead is also used when soldering components onto printed circuit cards. Antimony is often present, together with flame-retardants. This metal, and many of its compounds, are highly poisonous. Cadmium, which, together with nickel, is present in batteries and cathode ray tubes in TVs, and in computers, as a stabilizing agent in plastics, can accumulate in the body over the years and cause injuries to kidneys and other organs.

Flame-retardants are another group giving rise to problems. As early as 1992 Per Hedemalm, then at the Swedish Institute of Production Engineering Research in Gothenburg, warned that they would become the worst problem in this context. In the beginning of the 1990s it was already known that German workers involved in manufacturing plastics, who had come into direct contact with flame-retardants such as PBDE, polybrominated diphenylethers, had accumulated high levels of these substances in their blood.

The Germans were among the first to pay attention to the problems that electronic waste would cause in modern communities. They took the initiative on electronics regulations, based on producer responsibility. But the market reacted even before the regulations were made. It became almost impossible to sell a computer without a guarantee that it could be returned when it became worn out. The Germans were also first with respect to taking note of scrapped mobile phones, which contain, for example, cadmium, arsenic, beryllium, and mercury.

In a 1995 report *Waste from electrical and electronic products*, Per Hedemalm summarizes that the most serious risks of environmental effects from electrical product waste come from mercury and PCP (polychlorinated biphenyls) in old equipment, halogenated flame-retardants in plastic covers, cables and printed board assemblies, cadmium in nickel-cadmium batteries, and lead oxide in cathode ray tubes. He made a special note on the largely unknown material content of liquid crystal displays (LCDs) in flat-panel displays:

> More than 2000 different liquids can serve as liquid crystal materials in flat-panel displays. The amount of liquid is usually less than 1 dl in a 20 x 40 sq cm display. The formulas of these liquids are kept secret by the manufacturers and it has not been possible to get any data on the formulas used, nor of their health and environmental effects. The lamp used for backlighting usually contains mercury or rare earth metals. It has not been possible to get any information on the material content of the glass of LCDs.

"I didn't know that there are dangerous substances in electronic waste," said a Swedish Green Party local government commissioner during an interview for an article I wrote in 1996. This statement goes to show how great the lack of knowledge of the content of electronic waste has been, and, in many other countries, still is.

Many local government projects have been started in Sweden to recycle electronic waste. The purpose has often been to give employment to people who have been out of work for some time, disabled persons, immigrants, and refugees who find it difficult to get jobs. I have seen such workplaces where measures to protect employees' health have been non-existent. A brief training session on the first day at work and a few brochures have been all that was given to refugees and others before they started working. No tests, measurements, or medical examination have taken place. In an interview in a working environment journal, one refugee explained that he had learned that everything that looks like water is mercury, "and we have also got brochures that no one understands. Some of the people here are illiterate".

Now Sweden, too, has law regulations based on producer responsibility and the handling of electronic scrap has been concentrated in the hands of bigger and more serious players.

Doctors in company medical services have a tendency to explain away possible health risks by referring to the fact that there has not yet been enough research. On the other hand, chemists and toxicologists stress that it is important to follow the principle of prudent avoidance, and not to wait for research results about very complex, interactive, biological processes. Reducing exposure at once is necessary.

Occupational health inspectors were completely unaware of hazards of this type of workplace only a few years ago. What happens in such work environments if, for example, a capacitor that contains PCB or cadmium breaks? In many cases there is no label giving information about whether or not capacitors contain PCB. It is estimated that 40 per cent of all capacitors contain PCB, despite these substances being banned in Sweden. In principle, Swedish manufacturers are not allowed to import capacitors or other components that contain PCB, but import still takes place via agents. PCB is also present in relays and batteries. On the rubbish dump, a capacitor that contains PCB is a tiny environmental bomb, which, sooner or later, will be triggered as the thin outer casing of plastic and aluminum breaks down.

Knowledge of the spread of halogenated (chlorinated or brominated) flame-retardants via waste is still insufficient. No checking has taken place, not even random inspection, when cathode ray tubes have been imported into Sweden from places like Taiwan and South Korea. No one has had time to think about health aspects in relation to electronics in the rush towards technological development. The only concern that has been taken seriously is that cathode ray tubes must not implode.

One of the most responsible players in this sector is the private company Stena-Technoworld, earlier called Crec, an abbreviation for computer recycling. This was one of the first companies of its kind in Scandinavia. Right from the start they have had the vision of taking responsibility for handling electronic waste in such a way that it does not harm the environment, nor employees in the plant. No matter how careful they have been, the company has not been entirely successful in this respect. In the early stages a problem arose with a fragmenting machine for printed circuit cards, cables, plastic covers, etc. Dust spread in the premises and gave rise to various symptoms such as skin irritations. The managers, some of who had previously been employed by Nokia, were well aware of what dust from printed circuit cards contain. So, they tried to make each working operation as safe as possible, even though this was not required by anyone. Work inspectors and practitioners in occupational medicine thought that it was perfectly acceptable to work without taking special precautions. Employees at this exemplary plant had levels of the highly brominated flame retardant BDE-183 in their blood 70 times higher than a control group of cleaning staff. This was shown in a study carried out by Professor Åke Bergman at Stockholm University. His findings resulted in better working conditions in the factory. Today the employees use clothing covering the whole body to stop uptake of chemicals via the skin. Something also for office workers to think about?

References

Allen, H. & Kaidbey, K., 'Persistent Photosensitivity Following Occupational Exposure to Epoxy Resin' *Arch. Dermatol.*, Vol. 115 (Nov. 1979)

Becker, R. O., *Cross Currents*, Bloomsbury, 1990

Bergqvist, U. & Vogel, E., 'Possible health implications of subjective symptoms and electromagnetic fields, A report prepared by a European group of experts for the European Commission' DG V. *Arbetslivsinstitutet*, 19, (1997)

Bergqvist, U., Hillert, L. & Birke, E., 'Lägesrapport. Elöverkänslighet och hälsorisker av elektriska och magnetiska fält. Forskningsöversikt och utvärdering' *Rådet för arbetslivsforskning*, RALF, (March 2000)

Bergqvist, U., Hillert, L. & Birke, E., 'Elöverkänslighet – kunskap och erfarenheter.' *Rådet för arbetslivsforskning*, RALF, (2000)

Brodeur, P., *Currents of death*, Simon and Schuster, 1989

Carlo, G. & Schram, M., *Cell Phones, invisible Hazards in the Wireless Age*, Carrol & Graf Publishers, Inc., 2001

Carlsson, H., 'Polycyclic Aromatic Nitrogen Heterocyclics and Organophosphate Esters, Analytical Methodology and Occurrence in Occupational Environment' Department of Analytical Chemistry, Stockholm University, 1999

Colborn, T., Dumanoski, D. & Peterson, M., *Our stolen future*,

Abacus, 1996

Cutz, A., 'Effects of microwave radiation on the eye: The occupational health perspective' *Lens and eye toxicity research*, 6 (1 & 2), (1989), 379–86

Daily, L. et al., 'The effects of microwave diathermy on the eye' *Am. J. Ophth.*, 35 (1952), 1001

DeMatteo, B., *Terminal shock, the Health Hazards of Video Display Terminals*, NC Press Limited, Toronto, 1986

Fews, A. P., Henshaw, D.L., Keitch, P.A., Close, J. J. & Wilding, R. J., 'Increased exposure to pollutant aerosols under high voltage power lines' *Int. Radiat. Biol.*, (1999)

Forshufvud, R., *Bostad och hälsa*, Mimers Brunn förlag, 1998

Frey, A. H., 'Headaches from Cellular Telephones' *Environmental Health Perspectives*, (March 1998)

From Witchcraft to Science, a report from two seminars about hypersensitivity, Vårdalstiftelsens rapportserie No. 1, (2001)

Gangi, S. & Johansson, O., 'Skin changes in "screen dermatitis" versus classical uv- and ionizing irridation-related damage – similarities and differences. Two neuroscientists' speculative review.' *Exp. Dermatol.*, 6, (1997), 283–91

Gangi, S. & Johansson, O., 'A theoretical model based upon mast cells and histamine to explain the recently proclaimed sensitivity to electric and/or magnetic fields in humans' *Med. Hypotheses*, 54 (2000), 663–71

Gibson Reed, P., *Multiple Chemical Sensitivity*, New Harbinger Publications, Inc., 2000

Göransson, K., Andersson, R., Andersson, G., Marklund, S., Andersson, K., Östby, P. & Zingmark, P-A., 'An outbreak of occupational photodermatosis of the face in a factory in northern Sweden' Proc. 3rd International Conference Indoor Air Quality and Climate, Stockholm 1984, vol. 3, p.367

Hallberg, Ö. & Johansson, O., 'Melanoma incidence and frequency modulation (FM) broadcasting' *Archives of Environmental Health*, 57 (2002), 32–40

Hallberg, Ö. & Johansson, O., 'Cancer trends during the 20th century' *J. Aust. Coll. Nutr. & Env. Med.*, 21 (2002), 3–8

Hanson Mild, Kjell, Hardell, Lennart, Kundi, Michael, and Mattsson, Mats-Olof, Mobile telephones and cancer: Is there really no evidence of an association? *International Journal of Molecular Medicine* 12 (2003): 67–72

Hardell, L., Näsman, Ö., Påhlsson, A., Hallqvist, A. & Hanson Mild, K., 'Use of cellular telephones and the risk for brain tumours: A case-control study' *Int. J. Oncology*, 15 (1999), 113–6

Hardell, L., Eriksson, M., Lindström, G., van Bavel, B., Linde, A., Carlberg, M. & Liljegren, G., 'Case-control study on concentrations of organohalogen compounds and titers of antibodies to Epstein-Barr virus antigens in the etiology of non-Hodgkin lymphoma' *Leukemia and Lymphoma*, 42 (2001), 619–29

Hardell, Lennart, van Bavel, Bert, Lindström,Gunilla,Carlberg, Michael, Dreifaldt, Charlotte, Wijkström, Hans, Starkhammar, Hans, Eriksson, Mikael, Hallquist, Arne and Kolmert, Torgny, Increased concentrations of Polychlorinated Biphenyls, Hexachlorobenzene, and Chlordanes in Mothers of Men with Testicular Cancer, *Environmental Health Perspectives*, Vol 111, 7 (June 2003), 930–934

Hedemalm, P., 'Waste from electrical and electronic products, a survey of the contents of materials and hazardous substances in electric and electronic products' *Tema Nord.*, (1995), 554

Hedemalm, P., Eklund, A., Bloom, R. & Höggström, J., 'Halogenerade flamskyddsmedel i elektriskt och elektroniskt avfall. Förekomst och spridning i Sverige' *Naturvårdsverket*, (1999)

Henshaw, D. L., Ross, A. N., Fews, A. P. & Preece, A. W., 'Enhanced deposition of radon daughters nuclei in the vicinity of power frequency electromagnetic fields' *Int. J. Radiat. Biol.*, (1996)

Hilliges, M., Wang, L. & Johansson, O., 'Ultrastructural evidence for nerve fibres within all vital layers of the human epidermis' *J. Invest. Dermat.*, 104 (1995), 134–137

Hocking, B., 'Preliminary report; symptoms associated with mobile phone use' *Occup. Med.*, 48 (1998), 357–60

Hocking, B. & Westerman, R., 'Neurological abnormalities associated with mobile phones' *Occup. Med.*, 50 (2000), 366–8

Hocking, B. & Westerman, R., 'Neurological effects of radiofrequency radiation' *Occup. Med.*, 53 (2003), 123–7

Hollander, E., *The* TCO *enviro-labelling in* IT – *a case study of demand shaping and union proactivity*, written for EU DG XIII SPHERE-project.

Jacobi, H. H. & Johansson, O., 'Human dendritic mast cells' in: *Mast Cells and Basophils* (eds. G. Marone, L. M. Lichtenstein, S. J. Galli), San Diego, Academic Press, 2000, pp.89–95

Johansson, O., Hilliges, M., Bjornhagen, V. & Hall, K., 'Skin changes in patients claiming to suffer from "screen dermatitis": a two-case open-field provocation study' *Exp. Dermatol.*, 3 (1994), 234–8

Johansson, O., Virtanen, M. & Hilliges, M., 'Histaminergic nerves demonstrated in the skin. A new direct mode of neurogenic inflammation?' *Exp. Dermatol.*, 4 (1995), 93–6

Johansson, O., 'Elöverkänslighet samt överkänslighet mot mobiltelefoner: Resultat från en dubbel-blind provokationsstudie av metodstudiekaraktär, Enheten för Experimentell Dermatologi, Karolinska Institutet, Stockholm, Rapport nr 2, ISSN 1400–6111, 1995

Johansson, O., Liu P-Y., ' "Electrosensitivity", "electrosupersensitivi ty" and "screen dermatitis": Preliminary observations from ongoing studies in the human skin.' in *Proceedings of the COST 244, Biomedical Effects of Electromagnetic Fields – Workshop on Electromagnetic Hypersensitivity* (ed. D Simunic), Brussels/Graz, EU/EC (DG XIII),1995, pp.52–7

Johansson, O., Hilliges, M. & Han S. W., 'A screening of skin changes with special emphasis on neurochemical marker antibody evaluation in patients claiming to suffer from screen dermatitis as compared to normal healthy controls' *Exp. Derm.*, 5 (1996), 279–85

Johansson, O., Liu, P-Y., Bondesson, L., Nordlind, K., Olsson, M. J., Lontz, W., Verhofstad, A., Liang, Y. & Gangi, S., 'A serotoninlike immunoreactivity is present in human cutaneous melanocytes'

J. Invest. Dermat., 111 (1998), 1010—4

Johansson, O. & Liu-P-Y., 'No differences found by immunohistochemical screening of certain neuropeptides in patients suffering from so-called screen dermatitis' Enheten för Experimentell Dermatologi, Karolinska Institutet, Stockholm, Rapport nr 3, ISSN 1400—6111, 1998

Johansson, O., Wang, L., Hilliges, M. & Liang, Y., 'Intraepidermal nerves in human skin: PGP 9.5 immunohistochemistry with special reference to the nerve density in skin from different body regions' *J. Peripher. Nerv. Syst.*, 4 (1999), 45—52

Johansson, O., Liu. P-Y., Enhamre, A. & Wetterberg, L., 'A case of extreme and general cutaneous light sensitivity in combination with so called screen dermatitis and electrosensitivity — a successful rehabilitation after vitamin A treatment — a case report' *J. Aust. Coll. Nutr. & Env. Med.*, 18 (1999), 13—6

Johansson, O., Fantini, F. & Hu, H., 'Neuronal structural proteins, transmitters, transmitter enzymes and neuropeptides in human Meissner's corpuscles: a reappraisal using immunohistochemistry' *Arch. Dermatol. Res.*, 291 (1999), 419—24

Johansson, O., Gangi, S., Liang, Y., Yoshimura, K., Jing, C. & Liu, P-Y., 'Cutaneous mast cells are altered in normal, healthy volunteers sitting in front of ordinary TVs/PCs. Results from open field provocation experiments' *J. Cutan. Pathol.*, 28 (2001), 513—9

Johansson, O., 'Screen dermatitis and electrosensitivity: Preliminary observations in the human skin.' in *Proceedings of the conference "Electromagnetic Environments and Health in Buildings", May 16—17, 2002*, at the Royal College of Physicians, London, UK, in press

LaDou, Joseph, Ed. State of the Art Reviews, Occupational Medicine,

The Microelectronics Industry, January-March 1986, Hanley & Belfus, Inc.

Lai, H. & Singh, N. P., 'Acute low-intensity microwave exposure increases DNA single strand breaks in rat brain cells' *Bioelec-*

tromagnetics, (1995)

Lindström, G., Van Bavel, B., Hardell, L. & Liljegren, G., 'Identification of the flame-retardants polybrominated diphenyl ethers in adipose tissue from patients with non Hodgkins lymphoma in Sweden' *Oncology Reports* 4 (1997), 999–1000

Maguire, H. C., 'Experimental Photoallergic Contact Dermatitis to Bisphenol A' *Acta Derm. Venereol.*, Stockholm, (1998), 408–12

Navas-Acién, Ana, Pollán, Marina, Gustavsson, Per, Floderus, Birgitta, Plato, Nils, and Dosemeci, Mustafa, Interactive Effect of Chemical Substances and Occupational Electromagnetic Field Exposure on the Risk of Gliomas and Meningiomas in Swedish Men, *Cancer Epidemiology*, Vol 11 (December 2002), 1678–1683

Persson, B. R.R., Salford, L. G. & Brun, A., 'Blood–brain barrier permeability in rats exposed to electromagnetic fields used in wireless communication' *Wireless Networks* 3 (1997), 454–461 'Research on skin-related health problems in working life, an international evaluation' *Rådet för arbetslivsforskning*, RALF, (1996)

Rajkovic, V., Matavulj, M. & Johansson, O., 'Histological characteristics of cutaneous and thyroid mast cell populations in male rats exposed to power-frequency electromagnetic fields' to be submitted, 2003.

Salford, Leif G, Brun, Arne E, Eberhardt, Jacob L, Malmgren, Lars, and Persson, Bertil RR, Nerve Cell Damage in Mammalian Brain efter Exposure to Microwaves from GSM Mobile Phones, *Environmental Health Perspectives*, Vol 111 (2003), number 7

Slominski, A., Pisarchik, A., Semak, I., Sweatman, T., Wortsman, J., Szczesniewski, A., Slugocki, G., Mc Nulty, J., Kauser S., Tobin, D. J., Jing, C. & Johansson, O., 'Serotoninergic and melatoninergic systems are fully expressed in human skin' *FASEB Journal* express article 1.1096/fj.01–0952 fje, published on line April 23, 2002

Slominiski, A., Pisarchik, A., Semak, I., Sweatman, T., Wortsman,

J., Szczesniewski, A., Slugocki, G., McNulty, J., Kauser, S., Tobin, D. J., Jing, C. & Johansson, O., 'Serotoninergic and melatoninergic systems are fully expressed in human skin' *FASEB J.*, 16 (2002), 896–8

Stankovic, N., Johansson, O. & Hildebrand, C., 'Increased occurrence of PGP 9.5-immunoreactive epidermal Langerhans cells in rat plantar skin after sciatic nerve injury' *Cell Tissue Res.*, 298 (1999), 255–60

Stenberg, B., 'Office illness, the Worker, the Work and the Workplace' Umeå University Medical Dissertations, New Series No. 399, ISSN 0346–6612

Wang, I., Hilliges, M., Jernberg, T., Wiegleb-Edström, D. & Johansson, O., 'Protein gene product 9.5-immunoreactive nerve fibres and cells in human skin' *Cell Tissue Res.*, 261 (1990), 25–33

Williams, R. J. & Finch, E. D., 'Examination of the cornea following exposure to microwave radiation' *Aerospace Medicine*, (Apr 1974), 393–6

Yoshimura, K., Liang, Y., Kobayashi, K. & Johansson, O., 'Alteration of the Merkel cell number in the facial skin of human electrosensitive patients – a morphological study' to be submitted, 2003

Glossary

Aldehydes A group of chemical substances, including formaldehyde. Sensitizing and suspected of being carcinogenic.

Antimony Metal. In contact with acids can produce an extremely toxic gas. Occurs together with halogenated flame-retardants.

Barium Very poisonous metal, used in alloys and as pigment in paints and fluxing agents. Found in cathode ray tubes in screens.

Beryllium Used in manufacture of alloys, etc. Beryllium-copper alloys are used in electric switches. Highly toxic.

Bromine Pungent dark red volatile liquid. Poisonous if inhaled and caustic in contact with eyes or skin. Can cause itchiness, coughing, nose bleeding, headaches, and difficulty in breathing. If inhaled for some time causes tiredness, nausea, and asthma-like symptoms. Large amounts of bromine fumes can cause permanent eye injuries.

Brominated flame-retardants Brominated substances present in circuit boards and casings used for electronic devices. Includes PBB, PBDE, and TBBP-A, etc.

Dioxins Common term for a group of substances consisting of polychlorinated dibenzodioxins and polychlorinated dibenzofurans. Altogether about 210 similar substances. Some of them, especially 12 known as "the dirty dozen" are extremely toxic. Dioxins may be formed when scrapping PVC plastics by melting down or burning. Polybrominated dioxins are referred to when chlorine has been replaced by bromine.

Enzymes Proteins that start up and control metabolism.

Epichlorohydrin Volatile liquid used in production of epoxide (epoxy) resin. Harmful to inhale and in contact with eyes and skin. Can cause dizziness, headaches, and breathing difficulties. Causes itching, reddening, and blisters if in contact with skin.

Epidemiology Science concerned with the occurrence, transmission, and control of diseases.

Epoxy Can be used for bonding in paints and epoxy resins. Epoxy resins are used in the manufacture of epoxy plastics. Has been shown to cause skin tumors in animal experiments. Dust from epoxy can cause allergic reactions, at least in people who are already sensitive.

Erythema Reddening of the skin.

Free radicals Atoms, molecules, or parts of molecules that have a free, unpaired electron, i.e. a negatively charged atomic particle.

Micronutrients Substances such as vitamins or trace elements that are essential for healthy growth or development but only required in minute amounts.

Mitochondria The "power stations" in cells.

Myelin Insulation around nerves, rich in fat.

PBB Polybrominated biphenyls, a group of substances with similar structure to PCB. Used as additives in flame-retardants. Serious long-term health and environmental impact. Soluble in fats, bio-accumulative. Can form brominated dibenzodioxins and dibenzofuranes.

PBDE Polybrominated diphenyl ethers. Have been used as additives in flame-retardants, above all computer and TV casing. Different variants are deca-BDE, octa-BDE, and penta-BDE. Form brominated dibenzofurans when exposed to UV light. Quick to form brominated dibenzodioxins and dibenzofurans upon combustion.

PCB Polychlorinated biphenyls, generic name for numerous fat-soluble compounds that have low degradability and increase in concentration in food chains. Can be stored in the body.

Phosphorous Chemical element, present in numerous chemical compounds, some highly toxic. Has been used in pesticides and in manufacture of the nerve gas, sarin.

Phototoxicity Poisonous effect exhibited when an organism is first exposed to chemicals, then to light.

Psoralen Substance that makes skin sensitive to light. Used together with UV light in treatment of psoriasis and vitiligo/leucoderma.

PUVA Abbreviation for psoralen-ultra-violet-activity. Treatment for psoriasis and vitiligo. Patient takes psoralen tablets and is subjected to UV radiation treatment.

Strontium Metallic element. Strontium sulfide is found in luminous paints.

TBBA or TBBP-A Tetrabromobisphenol-A. Used as flame retardant, above all in printed circuit boards but also in encapsulation of components. The most common of all flame-retardants. Found above all in epoxy plastics. Can form brominated dibenzodioxins and dibenzofurans. Can have effect on thyroxine's function in the body.

Index